the KASAMBAHAY
child domestic work in the Philippines: a living experience

Ma. Cecilia Flores-Oebanda
Roland Romeo R. Pacis
Virgilio P. Montaño

Visayan Forum Foundation Inc.
International Labour Office
Manila, Philippines

Flores-Oebanda, Ma. Cecilia; Pacis, Roland Romeo R.; Montaño, Virgilio P.
The KASAMBAHAY
Child domestic workers in the Philippines: a living experience
Quezon City
International Labour Office 2001
ISBN No. 92-2-112697-8

Editor: Loree Cruz-Mante
Consultant: Ma. Teresa Camacho dela Cruz
Photos by Visayan Forum Foundation / Roland Pacis
Cover Illustration: Joanne de León

contents

v foreword

vii preface

ix ackowledgements

xi acronyms

1 part one: the phenomenon

3 **a look at the invisible**
the situation

9 **more than words**
the cultural context

17 **the big picture**
macro-view of the phenomenon

25 **scattered children, scattered laws**
existing legal framework

37 part two: up close

39 **re-examining roles**
the dynamics of their world

53 **not quite family, not quite employee**
their ambiguous role

59 **the dutiful child**
profile

65 part three: strategies

67 what works for filipino cdws?
development of the visayan forum's approaches

73 learning while living
synthesis of visayan forum strategies

77 not necessarily a welfare approach
direct services

89 from commodity to empowerment tool
education

95 planting seeds of their freedom
organising the sumapi

101 developing inner strength
resiliency building

107 tools for social change
advocacy, lobby work and networking

115 lobbying for policies and legislative framework
batas kasambahay

121 attacking the roots of the cdw issue
prevention work

127 part four: clarion call

129 a glimpse of the ocean
issues and challenges

143 to be treated as persons
recommendations

149 endnotes & bibliography

foreword

For so long, the plight of child domestic workers has continued to be hidden and unrecognized despite inceasing abuse and exploitation. Child domestic work is considered as one of the worst forms of child labor in the Philippines and is probably the most difficult to tackle considering the hidden nature of the job. It has been a widespread practice in different parts of the world and it may have worsened in recent years with the economic crises.

The emergence of a global movement against child labor has brought forward greater attention to the issues of child labor especially the elimination of its worst forms. The recent adoption and ratification in many countries of ILO Convention 182 Elimination of the Worst Forms of Child Labour is one of the concrete steps in the fight for its eradication.

The work of the Visayan Forum with child domestic workers is very commendable and worthy to emulate. The Visayan Forum takes a holistic approach to the issue of child domestic work - involving prevention, protection, withdrawal and integration - that has developed over time. The Visayan Forum, under the able leadership of Ms. Cecil Oebanda, tackles the root causes of the problem by working with community organizations, through mainstreaming the issue, for example, in enabling measures such as national legislation and cooperation with workers' organization.

Although there has been a growing awareness on the issue, still there is much to be done to make it a priority everywhere. There is an urgent need to initiate advocacy work and programs for children employed in domestic work recognizing that comprehensive and country specific policies and program responses need to be taken, comprising preventive and protective approaches at all levels.

This book on Kasambahay is an attempt to present successful strategies by an NGO partner of ILO-IPEC and bring added value in developing replicable models on child domestic work intervention. It is hoped that more concrete actions will be put forward to put emphasis on the work done by this group of silent workers. Let us give them the attention they long deserve.

WERNER KONRAD BLENK
Director
ILO Manila and Southeast Asia and
the Pacific Multidisciplinary Team

preface

This is a book about experience. It is not only about the issue of child domestic work in the Philippines: it offers more than just a systematic analysis of the phenomenon. It is rather a humble attempt to write down our experiences as a non-government organization or NGO that dared make a difference to the much-neglected and invisible plight of young domestic workers in our country, after being inspired into action by the Filipino domestic workers overseas. It is a continuing reflection on what we are doing with the help of domestic workers themselves, their employers, our government, and local as well as international civil society.

This book basically explores the Visayan Forum Foundation's experiences from an implementer's point of view. There are quite a number of studies and evaluations made by our partners and friends concerning our work; the feedback is usually that there is too much to absorb in so little time. On such occasions, we wanted to tell them more but could not, because we felt poorly equipped to study ourselves, to write our own experiences. Perhaps wrongly, we felt that we were better as implementers than as writers.

The actions we took in implementing the ILO-IPEC funded *Kasambahay* (household partner) Program since 1995 are merely small ripples in the ocean of misery of child domestic workers (CDWs). While many local initiatives existed in the past, many consider the work of the Visayan Forum as significant because it is a pioneering work. It has mobilized a critical mass. It has developed holistic intervention strategies. It is pro-active to the needs of the target group, grounded on experience, always in partnership with CDWs. The Visayan Forum also has a special role in drafting and popularizing *Batas Kasambahay*, a magna carta for Filipino domestic workers based mainly on its experiences with CDWs.

This book is therefore written for those who aim to be part of this catalytic process.

Yulenla

Ma. Cecilia Flores-Oebanda
President
Visayan Forum Foundation, Inc.

Authors' Note

Although there is a significant number of domestic workers who are men or boys, we refer to child domestic workers throughout this book in the feminine form ("she" and "her") as most of them are women or girls, and the job is predominantly associated with women's work. However, this is not to disregard the important contribution done by the males in this field.

acknowledgements

This book was made possible with the valuable support and assistance of our families, friends and partners. We cordially thank them all, especially the following for their special support:

All Visayan Forum staff and volunteers, both in Manila and in the regions, who are directly involved in program operations;

Our board members, especially Atty. Joaquin Garaygay, Lulu Zuñiga, and Engr. Elmer Cordero;

The International Labour Organization - International Programme on the Elimination of Child Labour (ILO-IPEC), for its support for the *Kasambahay* Program since 1995, especially the people who journeyed with us for the past 6 years: Thetis Mangahas, Amy Torres and Pin Boonpala;

Our international partners, especially Ute Karolus, Karin Oppowa and Maria Winiger of Caritas-Switzerland; Birgitta Ling of Save the Children-Sweden

Our non-government partner organizations, both local and international, especially in the Global March Against Child Labor movement;

Our government partners, especially in the Department of Labor and Employment (DOLE), Asec Rey Conferido, Chit Cilindro, and the staff of Institute for Labor Studies and the Bureau of Women and Young Workers-National Program Against Child Labor;

Child Workers in Asia and its network, especially its Board members and its Coordinator, Edel Silan; Victor Karunan; and Walter Skrobanek

Members of the Taskforce on Child Domestic Workers in Asia;

Anti-Slavery International;

Our *barkadas*: Beth Marcelino-de Castro, Agnes Camacho, Amihan Abueva and Teresa de la Cruz;

Loree Cruz-Mante for editing the manuscript;

The people whose pictures appeared in the section pages of this book;

All other child domestic workers who gave so much meaning to our lives;

And all who have in one way or another helped us in this publication. Truly, working with child domestic workers is not simply a job, but a personal commitment and partnering struggle.

Above all, we thank God with whom all things are possible.

Maraming Salamat!

Cecil, Roland and Vio
Manila, Philippines
2001

acronyms

ASI	Anti-Slavery International
BWYW	Bureau of Women and Young Workers
CDW	Child Domestic Worker
CLPMT	Child Labor Program Management Team
CWA	Child Workers in Asia
CWC	Council for the Welfare of Women and Children
DECS	Department of Education, Culture and Sports
DOLE	Department of Labor and Employment
DOJ	Department of Justice
DOT	Department of Tourism
DSWD	Department of Social Welfare and Development
ERDA	Education Research and Development Assistance
GO	Government Organization
ILC	International Labor Conference
ILO	Interational Labour Organization
IPEC	International Programme on the Elimination of Child Labour
LGU	Local Government Unit
NCUC	National City United Church
NBI	National Bureau of Investigation
NGO	Non-Government Organization
NSCB	National Statistical Coordination Board
NSO	National Statistics Office

OFW   Overseas Filipino Worker

PD   Presidential Decree

PGH-SSD   Philippine General Hospital - Social Services
            Department

PhilHealth Philippine Health Insurance Corporation

PO   People's Organization

RA   Republic Act

SBM   *Sagip Batang Manggagawa* (Rescue the Working
            Child)

SSS   Social Security System

STOP   Stop Trafficking of Pilipinos Foundation

SUMAPI   *Samahan at Ugnayan ng mga Manggagawang
            Pantahanan sa Pilipinas* or SUMAPI
            (Association and Linkage of Domestic
            Workers in the Philippines)

TDH   terre des hommes

UN   United Nations

UNCRC   United Nations Convention on the Rights of
            the Child

UNICEF   United Nations Children's Fund

VF   Visayan Forum Foundation, Inc.

part 1

the phenomenon

"...the combination of worsening socio-economic inequity — between the richest and poorest families, and between the rural and urban families — and an increasingly ill-fitting educational system is creating a vast labor pool of children."

a look
at the invisible

the situation

Child domestic work is one of the most disturbing features of Filipino life. It is disturbing because of its very nature — domestic work performed by a child, increasingly by very young girls, some as young as 8 years old, isolated and separated from their families. It is also disturbing because of the high incidence of deceptive recruitment and trafficking that characterize it. Finally, it is disturbing because of the very exploitative work conditions that also make these children vulnerable to sexual abuse.

Child domestic workers are statistically invisible.

Child domestic work is a massive, invisible engine of Filipino life. Domestic work is seen as dirty work that employers would rather have someone else carry out for them. As two-income households become more feasible and desirable, it also becomes more necessary to hire a domestic worker. As adults can often find better income in other forms of work here and abroad, domestic work falls more and more on children.

In 1995, the National Statistics Office found that there were at least 766,000 domestic workers in the Philippines. Of these, at least 301,701 were 19 years old or younger.[1] As the surveying government agency cautioned, however, these figures refer to paid domestic workers: this does not include children who work in exchange for room and board, or for the chance to study.

If each household in the highest income bracket alone (earning at least PhP250,000 a year or US$5,000*) in 1997 had only one domestic worker in their employ, then in that year, there were at least 1.395 million domestic workers in the country. Some households have approximately 6 domestic workers with specialized tasks (baby sitting, gardening, cooking, cleaning, washing and ironing, and driving). If the top upper class employed an average of only 2 domestic workers per household, there may be as many as 2.5 million domestic workers in the Philippines.

If the 1995 proportion remained consistent, then there were at least 549,490 domestic workers who were 19 years old or younger. Today, there may be as many as 1,098,980 child domestic workers in the country.

Note: $1 = PhP50

statistics

Philippine population: 75,329,000[2]

Population under 20: 34,757,911[3]

18% of the overall population of children between the ages of 5-17 work.[4] It is estimated that 55.7% of the country's working children are unpaid family workers, 38.2% are wage and salary workers, and 7.1% work on their own account.

86% of domestic workers 10-19 years old are female.[5]

409,851 children aged 5-17 are living and working away from home; among these, 256,826 are engaged in economic activities and housekeeping. Of these, 165,346 are girls.[6]

It is difficult to count how many child domestic workers there are. In the first place, labor force and employment statistics gathered by the government capture only those who are at least 15 years old.[7] In the second place, enterprises employing 10 or less are classified in the informal sector.[8] Nor is either domestic work or domestic workers included in the industries and occupations of the informal sector. In addition, employers and their domestic workers who are kin do not report employment, and neither do employers who pay their child domestic workers in the form of schooling or room and board instead of cash.

In short, child domestic workers are statistically invisible.

There are forms of child domestic work where children suffer grievous work that make them vulnerable to verbal, physical, and sexual abuse.

Child domestic workers work an average of 15 hours daily, and are on call 24 hours a day. Days off are limited to one day each month; many have no day-off at all. Confined to repetitive, menial work, most of these children have no opportunity to acquire life skills that would help them grow into productive adults.

Working away from her home, the child is separated from her family for extended periods of time. She and many others like her are prohibited from communicating with their families. The child is thus under the complete control of her employer, who does not necessarily serve the child's best interests. The child's freedom of movement is also limited. Many CDWs are not even allowed to venture beyond the house gates, except when the employer sends them on errands or brings them along when their services are needed. Isolated from family and peers, they rarely leave even when they suffer abuse. Thus, they are also literally invisible.

Isolated in the privacy of their employer's home, child domestic workers are literally invisible.

These children are among the lowest paid workers, receiving an average of PhP800 (US$16) a month — if paid at all. Few employers comply with the law requiring domestic workers earning more than PhP1,000 (US$20) a month to be registered for social security benefits. From this meager amount, CDWs frequently remit part of their income (when they receive any) to their family. Many also buy their own supplies, including medicine, and sometimes even their own food.

Some begin their working life in debt to recruiters who paid their transportation and lodging on the way to the employing household (two to three months' worth of the child's wages). Some employers sell clothes and other personal items to their domestic worker, who buys it rather than be accused of ingratitude, even when it takes months of going without a salary to pay for it. When an overtired child makes mistakes, some employers deduct the equivalent cost from her salary. When emergencies occur at home, the child domestic borrows from her employer, who also deducts the loan payment from her salary. The child is then trapped into debt, and thus into bondage. One CDW had to work off her debt for 2 years.

The childhood of child domestic workers is bought, paid for, and deducted from their very lives.

One can find CDWs escorting their employer's children to and from school as part of their duties, usually not as students themselves. Even when employers allow them to go to school, their heavy workload and long work hours — which are not adjusted for their schooling — disturb their studies, and they have no money for school-related expenses. Many are forced to drop out. Unable to acquire the means to better themselves, they drop out of their hopes and dreams as well.

CDWs often endure inhumane treatment. They suffer insults on a daily basis. Employers call them *tanga, gaga, bobo* (stupid), *batugan* (lazy), *tarantada* (careless), *walang pinag-aralan* (illiterate), *bastos* (rude), *malandi* (flirt), *sinungaling* (liar), and other derogatory names. A child who often hears these demeaning words would tend to believe these are true and thus lose her self-confidence and self-respect. An employer can easily jail CDWs merely by accusing them of theft. Without any immediate access to legal assistance, they can rot in jail until the case goes to court. They are usually lumped together as youth offenders. It is as though they are not citizens within the same legal system, as though they are invisible to the law.

Many are beaten, some even to the point of death. There are cases where the tormenting employer's creativity exempts his or her acts from being called beatings: one child domestic died from being forced to drink a liquid used to unplug drains. Another child was forced to drink bleaching liquid each time she failed to wash all the laundry, ostensibly as a form of discipline. One was made to kneel on a stool for hours, while balancing a fire extinguisher on her outstretched arms.

This is torture and brutality, not discipline by any stretch of the definition. These are not acts to provide anyone, even an adult, with a guide to improve performance or behavior: these are acts meant to injure, torment, and even kill.

Girls are sexually molested, usually when their duties include giving their employer a massage. Some are raped, after an escalating series of molestations. In Cebu City, the regional Department of Social Welfare and Development (DSWD) reveals that 80% of reported victims of rape, attempted rape and other acts of sexual abuse are child domestic workers.[9] These acts have no relation to the "personal comfort and convenience" defined by the

Article 14 of the Labor Code defines domestic or household service as "services in the employer's home which are usually necessary or desirable for the maintenance and enjoyment thereof, including ministering to the personal comfort and convenience of the members of the employer's household."

Labor Code: sexual molestation and rape are expressions of power over others, having nothing to do with sex.

Invisible and isolated, overworked and underpaid, deprived of the opportunity to study and to play, verbally abused day in and day out — this is how many child domestic workers live. In the worst situations, they are abused to the point of death and hopelessness. This is how perhaps 1,098,980 Filipino children live today. One million future adults — if they survive this kind of childhood.

It is a tribute to the resiliency of these children, as well as to concerned citizens and organizations, that many do survive. They somehow find in themselves the resolution to live. The courage to hope. The strength to insist on their humanity.

It is amazing how many CDWs are somehow able to go beyond their experience. They are blessed with the generosity to forgive, rather than hold on to hatred. Their ability to trust others has not been diminished, only sharpened by what they went through. Rather than seek revenge for the way they were treated, these children opt to focus their efforts on keeping other children and other child domestic workers from becoming the victims of what is conceded as part of the Filipino way of life, Filipino culture, and Filipino history.

case story: Rosie

Aged 14, Rosie's duties include, in addition to her household duties, caring for her employer's 14 breeding dogs. "The dogs are so big! I'm afraid to go near them. Every day I prepare kilos of dog food, wash out their pens, and take care of the mother dogs with newborn puppies. Sometimes I can't sleep properly for three nights running, for fear the puppies may die. All dogs are made in heaven, they say, but some domestics live in hell. My employer doesn't allow me to have any of the family's leftovers. I'm always hungry! Well, one day I couldn't tighten my belt anymore, so I ate the food of the dogs."

more than words

the cultural context

Previously, we have attempted to draw a picture on the phenomenon of child domestic work from existing studies. The hard numbers and case studies satisfy the need to understand the extent and magnitude of child domestic work in the Philippines. But the phenomenon also has historical and cultural roots, expressed today through our language.

We have various terms to refer to domestic workers. These terms do not exist apart from the reality: in fact, language represents real life. It can have a significant impact, either good or bad, on one's self-image. Hence the struggle for politically correct terms to ensure that the images words project are stripped of negative meaning. Sticks and stones break bones, and words injure or annihilate what defines us: one's self-esteem.

Consider the labels we use to refer to domestic workers. We usually call them *katulong* or helper, *alalay* or assistant. These words capture how society regards domestic work. On one hand, it is secondary, undesirable and marginal, for it is work that the domestic worker's employer cannot be totally bothered with. On the other hand, it is supportive and necessary to everything else that the employer does, for he has gone out and hired someone else to do it for him! This is exactly what domestic work is in the Philippines, although it may not be true in other countries, especially the industrialized ones.

Since domestic workers are widely accepted, affordable and accessible, employing them is a practice that is part of the everyday life of the Filipino household. You can hardly go to work in unwashed, wrinkled clothes, with no breakfast and no supper the night before. Your child or children can hardly be expected to go to and from school unattended. You cannot take the toddler to the office, and expect to be able to fulfill the demands of your job. You cannot be tied up in an important after-work meeting and run around buying groceries at the same time. You can hardly remember to take out the trash either in the morning as you rush to the office, or at night when you crawl home too tired to even smile.

> On one hand, it is secondary, undesirable and marginal, for it is work that the domestic worker's employer cannot be totally bothered with. On the other hand, it is supportive and necessary to everything else that the employer does, for he has gone out and hired someone else to do it for him!

Doing house chores is secondary, undesirable and marginal. As many full-time house-wives or house-husbands know, domestic work is sheer drudgery. You do the same things every day, some every week. Over and over again, every day, every week, of every month in every year. You arrange your work around your spouse's and children's schedules. On bad days, you identify with the worst of what you work on: dirty dishes, dirty laundry, dirty house, the trash. On really bad days, you identify your worth with the amount of money you bring into the household: none.

The low value society gives domestic work extends to the persons who do it. The terms *katulong* and *alalay* take on a wholly different meaning when used in the context of domestic work. As we in the Visayan Forum have observed in our interactions with CDWs, many of them are ashamed to be identified as and called *katulong*. They wince at the outright scorn expressed by the terms *tsimay* or *atsay* (corrupted Chinese terms for domestic workers which have downgrading connotation).

At the same time, notice how domestic workers refer to their employer. Although they call their employer "sir" or "ma'am," *kuya* (elder brother) or *ate* (elder sister) in face-to-face conversations, domestic workers refer to their employer as *amo*, literally "master," when speaking or writing about them. It is well to remind us of the quotation, "There can be no masters where there are no slaves." If there are masters, then, there are slaves: the domestic workers.

Employing a domestic worker is a socially accepted practice in thePhilippines, with slavery as its historical root. Before our country was colonized by Spain, our tribes had two kinds of what may be considered as the equivalent of domestic servants: *aliping namamahay* (domestic slaves who can own property) and *aliping saguiguilid* (domestic slaves who are household property). These slaves were often captives of war, or in debt to the tribe.

The Spanish era introduced various schemes to extract free labor from Filipinos. In the guise of *obras pias* (works of piety), Filipino women were conscripted as servants of

> Employing a domestic worker is a socially accepted practice in the Philippines, with slavery as its historical root.

clerics and officials of the colonial government. Women with religious aspirations were made to render domestic services for clergymen.

The rise of urban centers and cities also gave rise to the need for household help, "to give comfort to the employers' home for them to engage in other productive endeavors outside the home." The practice, begun by the elite both in their urban household and at their *hacienda* (rural estate), thus spread to the middle and lower classes where both spouses need to work to attain and/or maintain their chosen lifestyle. More recently, it is common to find domestic workers who began their career at a very young age in their own rural village.

Although there are indeed enlightened employers, there are those who are simply unaware. The experience of most of the CDWs we have dealt with at the Visayan Forum and the trends indicated by other studies show that child domestic work by its very nature has many practices similar to slavery.

Where there are masters, there are indeed slaves. In its second-to-worst form, child domestic work re-creates the *aliping saguiguilid* of the ancient tribes, slaves who were household property. But even slaves were considered assets to be judiciously expended. They had no freedom on their own, but were fed and watered and treated in such a way that they could effectively carry out their duties.

When CDWs are no longer treated in that nearly rational manner, when abuse in its different forms is all that they receive in exchange for all the work they give, that is the worst form of child domestic work. Children treated as less than persons, less than animals, and less than machines. The Visayan Forum finds no words that can express what the worst of employers think they are.

In the Labor Code, domestic workers are called domestic servants, perhaps to differentiate them from civil or public servants. The National Commission on the Filipino Language translates the word "servant" into *utusan* (errand runner), *alila* (slave), or *katulong sa bahay*

> The rise of urban centers and cities also gave rise to the need for household help, "to give comfort to the employers' home for them to engage in other productive endeavors outside the home." The practice, begun by the elite both in their urban household and at their hacienda (rural estate), thus spread to the middle and lower classes where both spouses need to work to attain and/or maintain their chosen lifestyle.

(helper in the house).[10] The last term is colloquially used by everyone.

The term *utusan*, however, refers to a person whose role is to be ordered about, to be given commands. No wonder CDWs can rest only when the employer can no longer think up a task for them (such as getting them a glass of water in the middle of the night). The term itself limits their existence to obeying orders and commands.

The term *alila* has additional connotations of degradation, including the ill treatment of child domestic workers. Household equipment, appliances and pets are better treated than many child domestic workers.

Inasmuch as the Labor Code defines domestic workers as domestic servants, and the government's own Commission on the Filipino Language translates "servant" as *utusan* and *alila*, one cannot avoid the conclusion that the government itself has unwittingly defined the role and status of domestic workers: to be ordered about, and to be degraded.

"... to be treated as persons..."
— a CDW

Whether we refer to them as *katulong, katabang, timbang, kabulig, tsimay, atsay, utusan or alila*, we are expressing the value we place not merely on their work, but the value we place on them as persons. None of these terms capture the fact that we are referring to persons, much less children.

Our laws call those who hire domestic workers "employers" and not "masters," not merely because they employ domestic workers, but also to define their value as persons: they are not "masters" of domestic workers with powers over life and death, but "employers" with a set of responsibilities and rights.

This is why the Visayan Forum advocates the term *kasambahay*, a contraction of *kasama sa bahay* (literally "companion at home"), or household partner. With this statement, we hope to build a new understanding and experience of domestic work. With this statement, we offer a benchmark for relationships between those who toil as domestic workers and those who employ them. With this statement, we encourage domestic workers and their employers to embark on partnerships. The term "househelper" as used in the Labor Code is synonymous to the term "domestic servant" and shall refer to any person, whether male or female, who renders services in and about the employer's home and which services are usually necessary or desirable for the maintenance and enjoyment thereof, and ministers exclusively to the personal comfort and enjoyment of the employer's family.[11]

Rather than being servants, domestic workers' responsibilities are not limited to performing household tasks, but in actual fact extend to managing the welfare of the employer's home, freeing the employer to move towards his or her strategic life goals. As a partnership, the relationship is one of mutual trust and respect. As a partnership, both parties cooperate to resolve problems. As a partnership, there is room for change and for growth.

In a partnership, diverging goals are accommodated: the employer's own example allows the domestic worker to work towards a better life situation, most likely a better job. In a partnership, shortcomings are workable challenges that can be hurdled with mutually agreeable measures: there is no slave, for there is no master. In a partnership, there is no place for abuse of any kind from either side: if the relationship no longer works, then it is adjusted, or else civilly dissolved.

The term *kasambahay* is thus laden with both socio-cultural and political agenda.

In place of devaluing domestic work and those who perform such work, the term *kasambahay* offers to recognize the dignity of domestic work and of domestic workers.

In place of belittling CDWs' perception of themselves, the term *kasambahay* proposes to encourage them to develop a profound and positive understanding of themselves, upon which they can build their daily lives.

In place of hamstringing the perception of domestic work to the silent and submissive performance of household tasks, it creates space for making decisions

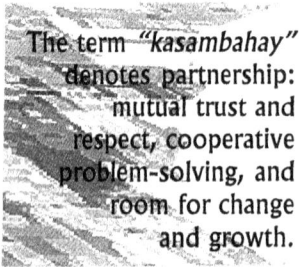

> The term *"kasambahay"* denotes partnership: mutual trust and respect, cooperative problem-solving, and room for change and growth.

within the bounds of an agreed-upon relationship, effectively giving them back their voice.

In place of the secondary, undesirable and marginal value society places on their work and on their persons, the term *kasambahay* reminds us of the supportive and necessary contribution domestic work and those who perform it provide our household, our lives, and our society.

"Being tired is just for a day,
but taking away your dignity will last forever,"
- anonymous CDW

the big picture

macro-view of the phenomenon

Although domestic servants have been a facet of Filipino life even in pre-colonial times, one would have thought that the technological developments of more recent times would have reduced the demand for household help. It appears, however, that technological developments have less to do with the continuing growth of domestic workers than do other factors.

According to the National Statistics Office 1997 Family Income and Expenditure Survey, while the average income of Filipino families showed a significant increase, only families belonging to the richest 10% registered an increase of 3.8 percentage points in their income share.

At the national level, the increase in average income seemed to keep pace with the increase in average expenses. However, this is true only for urban areas. In rural areas, the reverse was true: the increase in average expenditures outstripped increased income.

Average Increases (%) of Income and Expenditure, 1994-1997

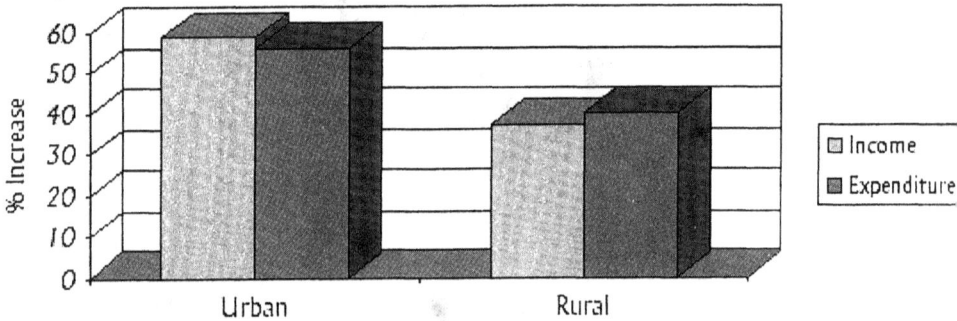

Regionally, the National Capital Region (NCR), Central Luzon and Southern Tagalog were still the top three regions in terms of average income posting estimates higher than the national average. Eastern Visayas, Central Mindanao, and the Autonomous Region of Muslim Mindanao had the lowest increases, with Eastern Visayas, posting estimates nearly half the national average, at the bottom of the heap.

The income distribution in 1997 became less equal (or more unequal) compared to 1994. In 1994, the average income of families belonging to the richest 10% of families was about 19 times higher than the average income of families in the poorest 10%. Put another way: for every peso earned by families in the poorest 10%, on the average, families belonging to the richest 10% earned PhP19.

This became worse in 1997: the average income of families belonging to the richest 10% of families increased to 23.8 times higher than the average income of families in the poorest 10%. That is, for every peso earned by families in the poorest 10%, on the average, families belonging to the richest 10% earned PhP23.80.

Average Income of Richest 10% and of Poorest 10%, 1994-1997

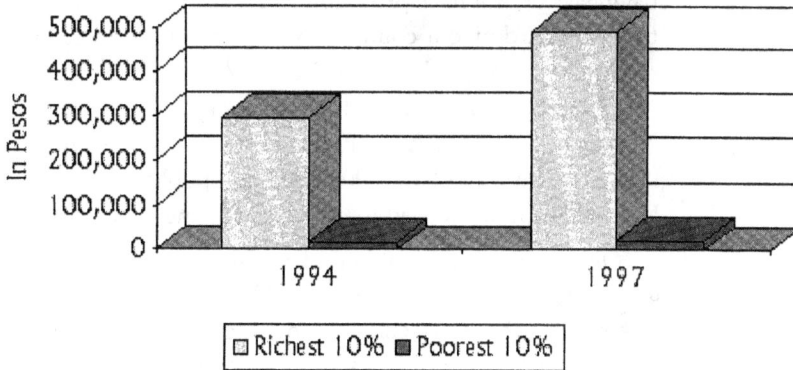

□ Richest 10% ■ Poorest 10%

Estimated average savings for the nation in 1997 came to PhP18,935 (US$378.70) net of inflation or more than one fifth (22.2%). This average amount is almost entirely in urban areas, though, because the average savings of rural areas is only PhP9,097 (US$181.94), or .4%. The increase in urban families' average savings was 55.5 times that of rural families. Put another way, for every additional peso that rural families saved in 1997 as compared to 1994, on the average, urban families saved PhP55.50.

When we look more closely by considering the richest and the poorest 10%, we find that the latter are posting increasingly negative savings, which may mean that they have had to borrow in order to support their expenditures. In 1994, the poorest 10% of families suffered a shortfall of PhP803.00 (US$16.06); in 1997, the shortfall had swelled to PhP2,393.00 (US$47.86).

Savings of the Richest 10% and the Poorest 10% in 1994 and 1997

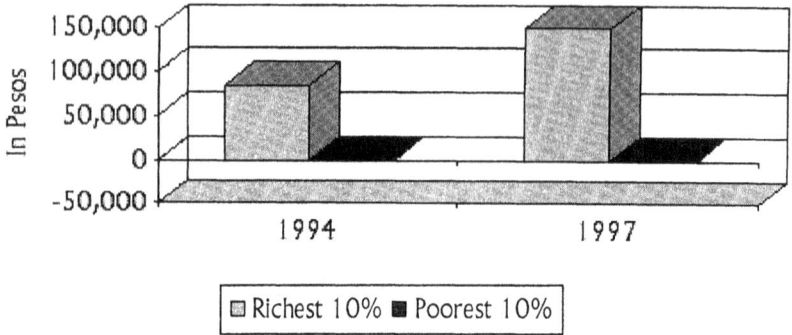

As recently as 1997, more than half of our country's barangays do not have provisions for a pre-school. More than one third of our country's barangays cannot offer the required 6 years of elementary education. In academic year 1999-2000, as many as 4,710 barangays do not even have an elementary school. Five towns do not have a high school.[12] This schoolyear 2001-2002, our public schools lack 8,000 rooms needed to accommodate new entrants.

Only 1 of every 5 children of pre-school age is able to go to public or private preschools. Although 97% of elementary school-age children do go to school, 60% drop out of school when they reach the second grade.[13] DECS Secretary Raul Roco is currently calling for donations, because 53% of all schoolchildren are in danger of dropping out due to lack of funds for uniforms and school supplies.

Secondary level schools attract only 65.4% of children who should be in high school. Only 23.9% of college-age youths participate in tertiary education.[14] According to the NSO (1994) out-of-school youths use their time in two different ways, differentiated by their sex: girls are occupied with housekeeping, while boys are working.

This combination of factors is why single, 15-year-old females migrate from poor agricultural or fishing communities in search of work. The participation of females more than 15 years of age in the labor force rises continuously. Although it slightly fluctuated to 48.2% in 1994 from 48.7% in 1989, female labor force participation rate jumped to a high of 50.2% in 1999.[15]

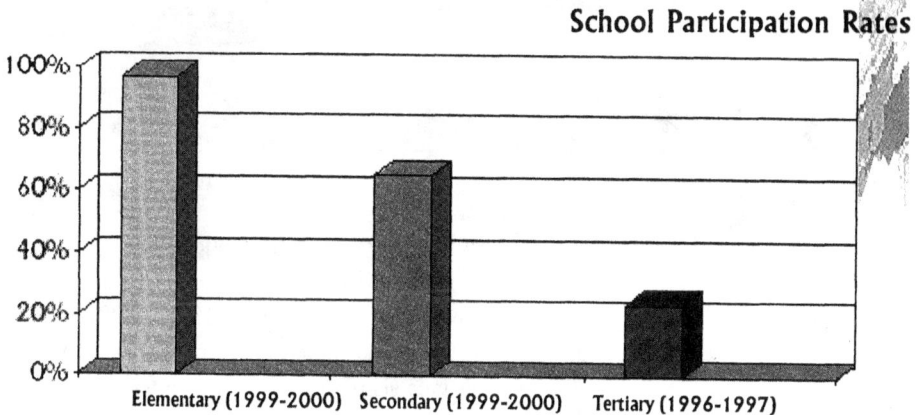

School Participation Rates

Elementary (1999-2000)   Secondary (1999-2000)   Tertiary (1996-1997)

And this despite the fact that the country has been suffering rising unemployment. In January 1999, 9% of the labor force could not find work; this rose to 9.5% in January 2000. This year, unemployment was pegged at 11.4% of the labor force . This is attributed by the NSO Philippine Labor Force Survey (January 2001) to the combined effect of the entry of additional persons into the labor force and the decline in agricultural employment. Employment is going down in the top two employing industries: agriculture, fishery and forestry (which employs 36.5% of our labor force) and community, social and personal services (which employs 19.1% of our labor force).

This may affect more men than women, although sex-segregated statistics for 2000-2001 are presently unavailable. Throughout the decade of 1989 to 1999, unemployed men outnumbered women. Men comprised more than half of the total unemployed persons while women accounted for declining proportions.[16]

In the period 1994-1999, women with gainful employment significantly increased by 3.9%, compared to only 2.7% among their male counterpart.[17]

Increase in Gainful Employment by Sex, 1994-1999

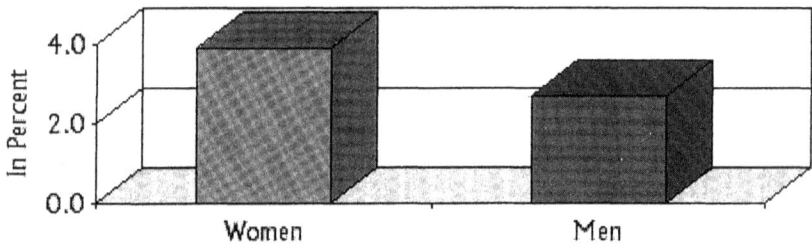

The services sector was the major employer of women throughout 1989 to 1999. It claimed more than half of the total in each study year (1989, 1994, 1999), while declining in the industrial and agricultural sectors.[18] In 2000, the service sector continued to post the biggest gain in employment (+3.6%). The sub-sectors which contributed the biggest gains were wholesale and retail trade (+4.7%) and community, social and personal services (+3.1%).[19]

Married women comprised more than half of the employed. In 1994-1999, with the reduction in the value of earnings of households due to increases in prices of basic commodities, an additional 4.8% (+257,600) among married women annually opted to work while single women grew by barely 1.5%.[20] This means that the market for domestic workers is also growing: 257,600 domestic workers may have been hired for these new vacancies every year.

From 1989-1999, more women were absorbed in better paying jobs, like in administrative, executive and

managerial positions. Wage and salary workers accounted
for the largest proportion of the employed (45.4% in 1989
and 47.9% in 1999). Own-account workers had almost
one-third of the total while the remaining were unpaid
family workers. Over the period, the first two groups of
workers posted increasing growth rates while the unpaid
family workers declined to 0.9% in 1994-1999 from 2.8%
in 1989-1994.[21]

Civil Status of Employed Women, 1994-1999

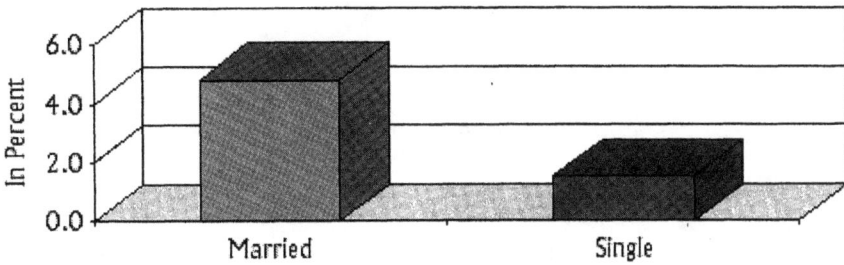

The sharp decline of female unpaid family workers
means, precisely, that there is a sharp decline of females
above 15 years of age working for their family without a
salary. They may have gone on to become wage and salary
workers or own-account workers, given the increasing
growth rates of these two occupational sectors. Who,
then, is filling the 257,600 vacancies for domestic workers
opened up every year? Most likely children below the 15
years cut-off of the labor force statistics.

In 1993, the United Nations revealed that 55% of the
total number of working children in Southeast Asia is to
be found in the Philippines.[22] In the Philippines, according
to the National Statistics Office survey last 1995, of every
20 children 18 years old or younger, 3 were already
working.[23] Around 3.7 million Filipino children work — to
help their parents, save for school, support themselves, or
simply to survive.[24]

On one hand, the combination of worsening socio-
economic inequity — between the richest and poorest
families, and between the rural and urban families — and

an increasingly ill-fitting educational system is creating a vast labor pool of children.

This vast labor pool of children is finding a willing market. Improvements in (mostly married) women's participation in the labor force, especially in well-paid work, is producing a demand for domestic workers. This demand can be addressed with advances in home technology. We can even consider reorganizing society to redistribute women's double burden of productive and reproductive work. Instead, this demand is being filled by children.

scattered children, scattered laws

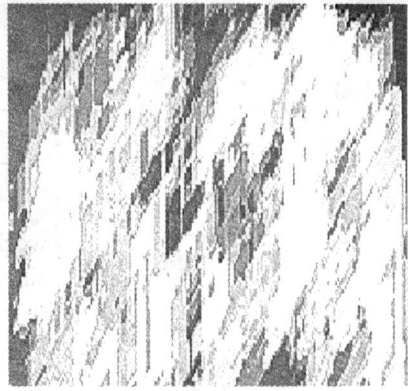

existing legal framework

Previously, we described the situation and context (social, historical and economic) of child domestic work in the Philippines. Have we no way to improve the situation of these children, and develop the practice so that these children are protected?

The Philippines has a strong legal framework on child protection. The 1987 Constitution declares the promotion of children's rights and welfare among its core beliefs. The National Program Against Child Labor 2000-2004 is geared towards "eliminating the worst forms of child labor and transforming the lives of child laborers, their families and communities, towards their sense of self-worth, empowerment and development."[25] The program focuses primarily on "preventing children from engaging in child labor, and ensuring that where children are found so engaged, they are provided protection and/or withdrawn from it, healed and reintegrated into a caring society."[26]

However, as various NGOs decried in our 1996 national consultation, laws that can conceivably be used specifically in favor of child domestic workers are few and far between. Only the legal blanket of Republic Act (RA) 7610 and its amended version RA 7658, together with Article 1691 of the Civil Code, Article 110 of Presidential Decree (PD) 603, and the Omnibus Rules Implementing the Labor Code (mandating compulsory elementary education for domestic workers), are directly helpful. As child domestic workers are literally scattered in private homes across the archipelago, the laws and issuances directly and specifically applicable to child domestic workers are also scattered among our laws.

The Labor Code contains generally applicable provisions concerning occupational safety and health. Article 14 defines domestic or household service as "services in the employer's home which are usually necessary or desirable for the maintenance and enjoyment thereof, including ministering to the personal comfort and convenience of the members of the employer's household." In addition, it prescribes wage standards and form; treatment; opportunity for education; board,

> As child domestic workers are literally scattered in private homes across the archipelago, the laws and issuances directly and specifically applicable to child domestic workers are also scattered among our laws.

lodging, and medical attendance; terms of termination; employment certification and records; and limits the range of duties in the employer's household. These are also defined in the Civil Code.

RA 7610 was enacted into law in 1992, "An Act Providing for Stronger Deterrence and Special Protection Against Child Abuse, Exploitation and Discrimination, Providing Penalties for Its Violation and For Other Purposes." Also known as the Special Protection of Children Against Child Abuse, Exploitation and Discrimination Act, it introduced innovative provisions for the protection of children in especially difficult circumstances. RA 7658, "An Act Prohibiting the Employment of Children Below 15 Years of Age in Public and Private Undertakings" was passed into law in October 1993, thereby restoring the erstwhile prohibition on the employment of children below 15 years of age.

RA 7655 sets standards for domestic workers' terms and conditions of work, including mandatory social security registration for those earning at least PhP1,000.00 (US$20). However, the legislated salary for domestic workers in the Labor Code is pegged at P800 (US$16) and this excludes them from benefiting from the Social Security System.

The Department of Labor and Employment's Order No. 4, series of 1999, defines hazards to working children, including child domestic workers, as follows:

- □ work which exposes children to physical, psychological or sexual abuse;
- □ work underground, underwater, at dangerous heights or at unguarded heights of two meters and above, or in confined places;
- □ work with dangerous machinery, equipment and tools, or which involves manual handling or transport of heavy loads;
- □ work in an unhealthy environment which may expose children to hazardous processes, to temperatures, noise levels or vibrations damaging to their health, to toxic, corrosive, poisonous, noxious, explosive, flammable and

combustible substances or composites, to harmful biological agents, or to other dangerous chemicals including pharmaceuticals; and

☐ work under particularly difficult conditions such as work for long hours or during the night, or work where the child is unreasonably confined to the premises of the employer.

The government also signed related international instruments, such as the United Nations 1989 Convention on the Rights of the Child. In ratifying this in 1990, the government recognized "the right of the child to be protected from economic exploitation and from performing any kind of work that is likely to be hazardous or to interfere with the child's education, or to be harmful to the child's health or physical, mental, spiritual, moral or social development." In the same act, it also committed itself to "take legislative, administrative, social and educational measures to ensure [its] implementation."

The International Labour Organization's 1973 Convention No. 138 (Minimum Age for Admission to Employment), is an instrument on child labor which is general in scope, and in principle covers all economic sectors and all employment or work, whether or not such work is performed under a contract of employment. Our country ratified it in 1998. ILO Convention No. 182, Concerning the Prohibition of and Immediate Action on the Worst Forms of Child Labor, was ratified in 2000.

Attempts to codify these scattered provisions for the benefit of CDWs, as well as for all domestic workers, have yet to be passed into law. The *Batas Kasambahay*, discussed in more detail later in the book, is the Visayan Forum's joint effort with others in enacting a Magna Carta for all domestic workers and their employers. Aside from codifying these provisions, the *Batas Kasambahay* also attempts to develop the law in accordance with our recognition of the domestic worker's value in our society, and of the fact that many of them are children.

> The *Batas Kasambahay*... attempts to develop the law in accordance with our recognition of the domestic worker's value in our society, and of the fact that many of them are children.

The recent ratification of ILO Convention No. 182 Concerning the Prohibition of and Immediate Action on the Worst Forms of Child Labor is only the beginning. The challenge today is identifying the conditions of child domestic work that threaten their life, safety, health and morals, or impair their normal development.

Aside from this, the Labor Code's provisions on working conditions and rest periods do not apply to "members of the family of the employer who are dependent on him for support, domestic helpers, persons in the personal service of another", among others. These are the provisions for:

- normal hours of work;
- meal periods;
- right to weekly rest day;
- right to service incentive leave;
- night shift differential;
- overtime work;
- computation of additional compensation;
- compensation for rest day, Sunday or holiday work;
- right to holiday pay;
- forms, time, place, and directness of payment;
- attorney's fees;
- non-interference in disposal of wages;
- allowable wage deductions;
- limitations on deposits for loss or damage;
- withholding of wages and kickbacks prohibited;
- prohibitions on deduction to ensure employment;
- retaliatory measures;
- false reporting; and
- eligibility for 13th-month pay.

The legal definition of "domestic or household service" itself is more of a catch-all phrase that utterly

> The challenge today is identifying the conditions of child domestic work that threaten their life, safety, health and morals, or impair their normal development.

fails to delineate any boundary whatsoever. As mentioned before, Article 14 of the Philippine Labor Code defines domestic or household service as "services in the employer's home which are usually necessary or desirable for the maintenance and enjoyment thereof, including ministering to the personal comfort and convenience of the members of the employer's household."

This is a dangerous definition. It is dangerous because it describes without delimiting; it explains without clarifying; it allows employers of domestic workers incredible and unparalleled leeway in interpreting what is actually part of the nation's laws. Any contract made on the basis of this definition can be misinterpreted and used to justify abusive treatment or actions.

The phrase "services in the employer's home which are usually necessary or desirable for the maintenance and enjoyment thereof" begs for a more specific list of "usually necessary or desirable services." As a result of this vagueness, most child domestic workers, save for those employed in multi-worker households where some degree of specialization is exercised, find themselves doing everything the employing household can come up with. In these children's own words, they are "all-around."

The phrase "ministering to the personal comfort and convenience of the members of the employer's household" practically waves a red flag saying "Hazard! Grounds for abuse!" We have already described how child domestic workers' work conditions make them vulnerable to sexual abuse. In these girls' own words, they are "like the employer's second wife."

The definition of "domestic servants" itself can be used to justify the treatment of child domestic workers as creatures to order about, or to demean. As something less than human.

Laws can, however, be only as good as their implementation. Although employers may be found responsible for violating the child domestic worker's rights, others who set up the situation for abuse are not. Whoever recruited the child — a relative, friend or

> Any contract made on the basis of the current definition (Article 14 of the Labor Code) of domestic or household service as "services in the employer's home which are usually necessary or desirable for the maintenance and enjoyment thereof, including ministering to the personal comfort and convenience of the members of the employer's household" can be misinterpreted and used to justify abusive treatment or actions.

townmate — cannot be held legally accountable for the child's fate at the hands of her employer. Unless recruitment was through a legitimate agency, the law has no means to regulate or monitor the trafficking of children for domestic work.

Agencies that are supposed to look after their rights as citizens, as workers, and as children face obstacles in implementing these laws. Even police are, understandably enough, wary of entering private homes without a warrant. And yet a way must be found to enforce the law, to protect these children's rights, to make these invisible children visible again.

The Visayan Forum believes that any law for the benefit of child domestic workers must build on the dynamics of the social actors involved — and these comprise our entire society.

As early as 1923, the Philippine government has sought to regulate child labor:

1923

The Inspection Division of the Bureau of Labor's Women and Child Labor Section was tasked to implement Republic Act (RA) 3071: "An Act to Regulate the Employment of Women and Children in Shops, Factories, Industrial, Agricultural, and Mercantile Establishments, and Other Places of Labor in the Philippine Islands."

1932

Revised Penal Code (RA 3815, as amended)
- prohibits slavery (Art. 272)
- prohibits exploitation of child labor (Art. 273) and
- prohibits exploitation of minors (Art. 278)

1952

RA 3071 was repealed by RA 679, "An Act to Regulate the Employment of Women and Children, to Provide Penalties for Violation Hereof, and for Other Purposes."

1957

The Women and Minors Division of the Bureau of Labor Standards started to administer and enforce RA 679, or the Bureau of Women and Child Labor Law, amending RA 3071.

1960

The Bureau of Women and Minors was created by virtue of RA 2714.

1973

Presidential Decree (PD) 148 amended RA 679, delimiting the employment of persons between 14 and 18 years of age to nonhazardous undertakings, and prohibiting the employment of children less than 14 years "except where the child works directly under the sole responsibility of his parent or guardian, involving activities which are not hazardous in nature and which do not in any way interfere with his schooling."

1974

Labor Code (PD 442) amended PD 148. It prescribes wage standards and form; treatment; opportunity for education; board, lo dging, and medical attendance; terms of termination; employment certification and records; limits the range of duties to the employer's household; these are also defined in the Civil Code. In addition, the Labor Code contains generally applicable provisions concerning occupational safety and health.

On December 10, PD 603 or the Child and Youth Welfare Code, codifying different provisions for the well-being of all children, was enacted into law. It protects the child against exploitation, improper influences, hazards and other conditions or circumstances prejudicial to his physical, mental, social and moral development. It also includes a host of other benefits for working children such as the duty of employers to submit reports and to keep a register of employed children, the right of working children to self-organization, welfare programs, etc.

1987

The Bureau of Women and Minors was renamed the Bureau of Women and Young Workers when the Ministry of Labor and Employment was reorganized.

1992

RA 7610 was enacted into law, "An Act Providing for Stronger Deterrence and Special Protection Against Child Abuse, Exploitation and Discrimination, Providing Penalties for Its Violation and For Other Purposes." Also known as the Special Protection of Children Against Child Abuse, Exploitation and Discrimination Act, it introduced innovative provisions for the protection of children in especially difficult circumstances, but legalized the employment of all children below 15 years of age, provided only that the employer first secures a work permit from the Department of Labor and Employment and ensures the protection of the child.

1993

RA 7658, "An Act Prohibiting the Employment of Children Below 15 Years of Age in Public and Private Undertakings" was passed into law in October 1993, thereby restoring the erstwhile prohibition on the employment of children below 15 years of age.

1995

RA 7875 or The National Health Insurance Act of 1995 (superseding PD 1519 or the Revised Philippine Medicare Act), created a National Health Insurance Fund under the administration of the newly established Philippine Health Insurance Corporation, from which members may secure essential goods, health and other social services at affordable cost.

RA 8282 or the new Social Security Law (amending RA 1161) provides to covered employees and their families protection against the hazards of disability, sickness, old age, and death, with a view to promoting their well-being in the spirit of social justice.

1999

Department of Labor and Employment Order No. 4, Series of 1999 stipulated that persons between 15 and 18 years of age may be allowed to engage in domestic or household service, as long as it does not endanger their life, safety, health and morals, or impair their normal development. It pinpointed the kinds of work that risk endangering children or impairing their development.

International instruments:

1953

ILO Convention No. 90: Night Work of Young Persons Employed in Industry, prohibits the employment of children in industry during night time. The term "night" signifies a period of at least 12 consecutive hours that includes the interval between 10:00 p.m. and 6:00 a.m. for children below 16 years of age, and a period that includes the interval of at least 7 consecutive hours between 10:00 p.m. and 7:00 a.m. for children between 16 and 18 years old.

1960

ILO Convention No. 59: Minimum Age for Admission of Children to Industrial Employment (revised), fixes the minimum age of employment for industry at 15 years but allows younger children to be employed in undertakings in which only members of the employer's family are employed, provided that such work is not dangerous to the life, health or morals of the children employed therein.

1960

ILO Convention No. 77: Medical Examination for Fitness for Employment in Industry of Children and Young Persons, requires the medical examination of children as a pre-requisite to employment and their subsequent re-examinations therein; also contains medical examination guidelines for different types of work for children.

1989

United Nations Convention on the Rights of the Child (UNCRC) states the right to protection from any work that is harmful to the child's health or physical, mental, spiritual, moral or social development. The rights the UNCRC expresses a model of childhood, which can be used as a benchmark. In addition to general rights to development, non-discrimination and respect for the child's best interests, there are a number of specific rights in the UNCRC that

CDWs do not, or may not, enjoy. These rights fall broadly into 6
categories of rights affecting CDWs: independent identity, selfhood,
and freedom; parental nurture and guidance; physical and
psychological well-being; educational development; psychosocial,
emotional and spiritual development; protection from exploitation,
including sexual exploitation, sale and trafficking.

1998

ILO Convention No. 138: Minimum Age for Admission to
Employment, an instrument on child labor which is general in scope,
and in principle covers all economic sectors and all employment or
work, whether or not such is performed under a contract of
employment.

1999

ILO Convention No. 182: Concerning the Prohibition of and
Immediate Action on the Worst Forms of Child Labor calls for
immediate and effective measures to secure the prohibition and
elimination of the worst forms of child labor as a matter of urgency.

part 2

up close

"For many CDWs, working in somebody else's home, especially their relatives, may be their only passport to a better life. It may be a second chance to have a good home, perhaps an opportunity to complete elementary education at least. It may be a haven from an abusive parent. It is the chance for regular meals, perhaps the opportunity to save for next semester's tuition fees, while the farm their parents till is stricken by drought or by civil strife."

re-examining roles

the dynamics of their world

The previous section tackled the situation of CDWs, as well as the social, historical, cultural, economic and legal backdrop of the phenomenon. We have sought to show that the phenomenon of child domestic work is not isolated, but is woven into societal problems. Because of its magnitude and intricate relationship with other societal issues, any effort to address it requires an approach that involves society as a whole — both political and civil society, and not merely on a local but on an international scale. Ultimately, society as a whole must address the issue of domestic work.

In this context, it is important to re-examine the roles of significant people in the life of a child domestic worker. The following diagram shows the various actors that affect the relationship between the child domestic worker and her employing household.

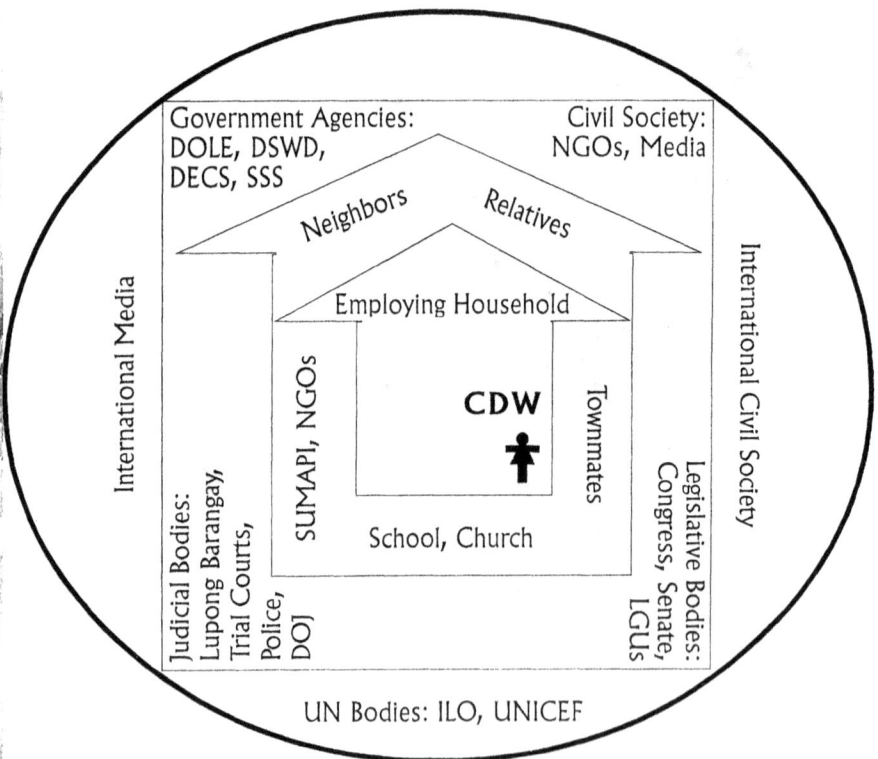

The CDW employer

It is difficult to generalize about the relationship between employers and their child domestic workers. There are employers who are very exploitative and abusive of their CDWs, but there are also those who support or are even exploited or abused by some CDWs. Whatever the quality of their relationship is, one thing is clear: they each play a vital role in the other's life.

Nothing can be done to improve the situation of child domestic workers unless those responsible for employing them are involved. [27]

Employers of child domestic workers are often active church-goers from two-income middle-class households. Many indicate that their hired help is part of the family more than she is an employee. In its best form, the family relationship between a CDW and her employer creates stronger bonds between them. It encourages mutual trust, respect, and a recognition of familial responsibility toward each other.

> Nothing can be done to improve the situation of child domestic workers unless those responsible for employing them are involved.

The more successful employers are those who are more realistic in their expectations of their child domestic worker. These employers keep firmly in mind that they employ children, not adults. They often shoulder the responsibility of ensuring that the domestic worker's childhood is not sacrificed.

Employers reached by the Visayan Forum permit their CDW to participate in the program. In addition, they themselves participate in the employers' orientation; share materials and goods with the program, especially during Christmas; and promote or endorse the program among their neighbors and contacts. These employers spot and report cases of CDW abuse that they uncover through their own network of friends, neighbors, and business associates. In the past, some have even absorbed child domestic workers who were either rescued from a dangerous situation, or needed temporary shelter for some other reason.

Political society, in the form of the government and its various branches and agencies, defines, implements, and monitors the legal terms of child employment in domestic work.

Judiciary

Based on media reports, the judicial system stands to benefit from a deeper understanding of the phenomenon of child domestic work. There were cases involving prominent people but were dismissed for lack of merit, without even having the victim's side heard in open court. In our experience, there was the case of a CDW who accused her employer of forcing her to drink an acid. The CDW died after filing the case in court. But the case, too, was dismissed for lack of evidence.

The judiciary is part of the audience whose awareness the Visayan Forum seeks to raise. It is necessary to change its perceptions, sensitize it to the situation of CDWs, and thus develop its sympathy for child domestic workers. Without this sensitivity, the preference of the judicial system for factual corroborated evidence and respect for employers' reputation can be — and actually is — used against the child domestic worker, who has only her testimony and her courage.

Legislature

In our work, we have found it necessary to have a well thought-out legislative advocacy plan. For example, the House of Representatives has been attempting to pass legislation that addresses domestic work and domestic workers, one of which is *Batas Kasambahay*. The work of the legislature and the judiciary are crucial in defining the acceptable relationship between employers and their domestic workers — the legislature through legislation, and the judiciary through the interpretation of the law in specific cases.

Law Enforcement

The local *barangay* (village) is the first recourse for child domestic workers in distress. According to the law, every Filipino has the right to free legal counsel. To provide this, there is a *Katarungang Pambarangay* (Village Court) in every village, which mediates between CDWs and their employers. The police provide assistance, and report cases of CDW abuse. Port police and Coast Guard officers are actively involved against trafficking. Labor inspectors mediate in labor cases in accordance with the Department of Labor and Employment's (DOLE) order regarding child labor. The National Bureau of Investigation (NBI) aids in initial investigation, and provides protective custody. The Department of Justice (DOJ) accommodates legal cases.

Government agencies

The DOLE assists in rescuing abused CDWs. It chairs the National Program Against Child Labor. It develops and strengthens government policies and programs on child labor, which include CDWs. It provides input on protection and welfare laws. The DOLE engages in advocacy through the development and dissemination of informative and educational materials among its regional offices and partner agencies. This effort includes popular materials such as comics and posters, as well as a primer on the rights of domestic workers. It conducts research and action programs, such as the 1995 Bureau of Young Women Workers' Project on the Working and Living Conditions of Young Domestic Workers. The DOLE is also institutionalizing and networking for the protection of child laborers, including its project the *Sagip Batang Manggagawa* (SBM), and the Child Labor Program Management Team (CLPMT).

The Department of Health provides free medicine and consultations in government hospitals, especially the Philippine General Hospital (PGH), which has a Child Protection Unit. The Social Services Department (SSD) of the PGH handles referrals of children abused during work. It liaises with the Department of Social Welfare and Development (DSWD), and the Visayan Forum as well, to provide shelter for children in need. PGH-SSD assesses abused children, and gives them medical assistance and counseling where appropriate. It refers these cases to the DSWD and the police department, as needed.

In turn, the DSWD provides protective custody, aside from rehabilitation and skills training for children rescued from domestic work abuse. It also assists CDWs returning to their families with its Back to the Provinces Program. Furthermore, it makes financial benefits available to particularly needy families. It is further tasked to coordinate line agencies working with child domestic workers.

The Department of Education, Culture, and Sports (DECS) offers specialized placement tests for child domestic workers who want to pursue their studies. This facility is unique to our country. Essentially, the child who stopped attending school long enough so that she is older than is usual for her grade level, has the opportunity to catch up with her peers, thereby minimizing the gap and making up for lost years. The DECS also supports institutions that offer educational programs for CDWs.

The Department of Tourism (DOT) issues permits to allow the Visayan Forum to hold outreach activities in parks, and assists program staff during Sunday gatherings.

The Council for the Welfare of Women and Children (CWC) is the agency responsible for monitoring and coordinating all activities on behalf of children. It is also responsible for policy formulation.

The Social Security System (SSS)

The Social Security System protects child workers in the form of benefits and privileges, extending social security coverage to CDWs as mandated by law. In recognition of child domestic workers' hours, it has redefined its outreach services since 2000, by extending its services beyond normal office days (Monday through Friday), and even beyond their office hours and outside their office buildings. For example, they have made this service available at the parks and schools where domestic workers can be found in significant numbers. It also educates employers on the importance of providing social security coverage and protection for child domestic workers, and follows up employers who violate the social security law (in terms of reporting and remitting contributions). In addition, the SSS conducts information campaigns, and maintains coordination with other relevant government agencies.

Civil society, in the form of institutions, organizations and concerned citizens, addresses child domestic work in various ways.

The Church

Some churches and organizations have lay apostolate programs for helping employer-domestic worker relations. Churches and other religious organizations, such as the National City United Church (NCUC) and the Catholic parish church of Batangas City, are influential on the employers of CDWs. They counsel and mediate between these children and their employers. They conduct values education sessions for domestic workers and their employers. Some also help in rescuing the children. They engage in advocacy through radio stations, parish newsletters, Bible studies, prayer brigades, homilies and sermons. They sponsor liturgical services honoring domestic workers, and hold specially-designed prayer events specifically for intentions of CDWs. They also make their facilities available for meetings, sponsor skills training and educational and recreational activities, and generate donations of educational supplies for child domestic workers.

The School

CDWs who are able to go to school often seek advice and help from their teachers. The school is the child domestic worker's second home, with their teachers taking on the role of surrogate parents, especially when the child's employer does not take up such a function. As surrogate parents, these teachers periodically check on the child's welfare. Individually, through the parent-teacher association, and sometimes institutionally, these teachers and/or schools provide counseling for CDWs, and assist them in negotiating with employers. Some assist in rescue and referral; some provide legal advice. They also refer student volunteers to help the Visayan Forum's *Kasambahay* Program.

Schools that accommodate child domestic workers, notably Assumption College of Davao, also create and provide alternative education schemes for these working children, such as Sunday school, night school, or distance education. They also offer vocational skills training, while others provide empowerment training on topics such as theater arts, leadership, organizing, and child protection laws. They adapt the national syllabus to child domestic workers' needs, and assist in making modules and translating laws. In addition, they are good venues for outreach activities, making their space and facilities available upon request.

The Media

The *Bantay Bata* of ABS-CBN-2 and The Probe Team of GMA-7 demonstrated the positive role media can play when they increased media exposure through a series of television programs on child labor issues. The broadcast of the video-documentary on CDWs, *Nakatagong Kasambahay* (English title: Out of Sight, Out of Mind), gave rise to different reactions and awakened public attention. The print media has also given a great deal of coverage to activities, projecting the issue further into the public awareness. In addition, CDW speakers have participated in media events as part of their advocacy. Broadcast media, both radio and television, has also served as a communication line between child domestic workers and their parents through public announcements, especially in remote areas.

Non-government organizations (NGOs)

Various non-government organizations in Manila and other regional centers, are involved in different ways. Some of these (mainly Metro Manila based) are:

☐ *Bantay-Bata,* part of the ABS-CBN Foundation, runs a program of activities dealing with the rights and needs of children in difficult circumstances. These include a 24-hour hotline throughout the whole country; a community program with medical and dental camps; a scholarship program for children;

family therapy; and rescue and referral
assistance.

☐ Stop Trafficking of Pilipinos Foundation
(STOP) offers livelihood training for adults to
improve family income and therefore lessen
the need to send children into labor. It also
engages networking for micro-finance for
families and for education possibilities for
children removed from the worst forms of
child labor.

☐ The Education Research and Development
Assistance (ERDA) offers direct educational
assistance to children in need.

☐ The Ateneo Human Rights Center's *Adhikain
para sa Karapatang Pambata* (AKAP) Program
offers legal assistance to CDW abuse cases
and provides seminars/trainings on child
labor laws and legal matters.

More NGOs contribute by referring CDWs to other
organizations that offer direct services, while others
engage in advocacy.

People's organizations (POs)

Workers' organizations have their own important role.
Because of their recognized mandate to fight for the
rights of workers, they can be effective in the fight against
child labor at the national level. Even at the international
level, workers' organizations as part of the tripartite
community of labor can bring the experience and inputs
of NGOs to international bodies and influence the
development of effective strategies. They are in a good
position to examine the ILO's core standards, for
example.

The *Bantay-Bata sa Komunidad* (Community Child
Watch) grew out of the Visayan Forum's community-
based approach to child domestic work. While identifying
the communities that CDWs hail from (also called sending
or source communities), we found that these communities
were concerned about the children who enter domestic
work at such a young age, and sometimes are never heard

from again. These communities monitor the recruitment or arrival and status of CDWs, and extend on-site assistance, often with the involvement of the child's own family.

The child domestic workers we reached established their own organization, the *Samahan at Ugnayan ng mga Manggagawang Pantahanan sa Pilipinas* or SUMAPI (Association and Linkage of Domestic Workers in the Philippines). Through their own organization, member CDWs engage in nationwide outreach activities: raising public awareness of the rights and plight of child domestic workers; identifying, tracing and reaching even severely isolated CDWs; spotting, reporting, and monitoring CDWs suffering from abuse and other difficulties; negotiating with their employers; facilitating CDWs' access to available services; and strengthening each other's resilience.

Currently, there is no employers' organization. Should there be one, it would be a very large organization: 1.395 million members, if the top Philippine income class alone employs domestic workers. It would also be multi-industry in character, because the domestic work industry, being household-based, cuts across all industries.

Other concerned citizens

Parents and/or relatives of child domestic workers themselves report cases of CDWs in distress to the Visayan Forum's *Kasambahay* Program. They also assist in rescuing these children, accompany them during repatriation, help in filing and pursuing cases, and, last but not the least, provide emotional care and support.

Adult domestic workers are instrumental in identifying who and where child domestic workers are. They obtain the employer's permission for the CDW's participation in activities; accompany these children to those activities; report cases of abuse; assist in conducting orientation seminars, education and training and other promotional activities; provide peer counseling for CDWs, especially in workplaces program staff cannot normally reach; and share materials and goods with them.

Other working students enrolled in the same school as CDWs attend orientations and other program activities; help in distributing flyers and other advocacy materials in the school; promote the program among their family, neighbors, and friends; and participate in tutorial sessions organized by SUMAPI.

Working street children from urban poor migrant families, most of whom are members of the *Bantay-Bata sa Komunidad*, act as watch support network in detecting and/or reporting cases of abuse; help promote the program in the community; provide assistance during major activities; join the Sunday outreach programs, especially in organizing recreational activities for child domestic workers; and organize street drama presentations on the plight of these children, which are usually showcased during advocacy campaigns.

Workers from the informal sector (garment, construction, and factory workers, retail store helpers, and waiters), some of whom were former child domestic workers, take part in recreational activities at the park; attend the orientations and trainings conducted by the program; help promote the program among others and endorse their CDW acquaintances to the staff; and act as watch support network in detecting and/or reporting cases of abuse.

Student volunteers and researchers document the program and give feedback on the impact of the activities on the beneficiaries; serve as counselors in the process while doing research work; share basic knowledge, skills and values with the child domestic workers (such as literacy and numeracy); and assist in databasing the CDWs reached by the program.

The global scale of the effort necessary to act on child domestic work is evident in the fact that international organizations have taken up the cudgels to curb its worst forms.

International bodies and actions

The work of international bodies is a good indicator both of what is possible and what is still required in working against the hazardous forms of child labor. International bodies consist both of organizations like the International Labour Organization (ILO) and its International Programme on the Elimination of Child Labour (IPEC), UNICEF, Caritas-Switzerland, terre des hommes, Anti-Slavery International, as well as Child Workers in Asia. The ILO-IPEC works to assert its influence on governments — to ratify its conventions, and to enact country-owned laws, regulations and mechanisms to implement them.

The Visayan Forum became the Philippine Secretariat of the Global March Against Child Labour, which became instrumental in the International Labour Conference's (ILC) adoption of the new ILO Convention on the Worst Forms of Child Labor. Through the Global March, CDW issues were emphasized during deliberations on the new convention. A CDW advocate from the Visayan Forum served as spokesperson on behalf of the child core marchers during the plenary of the ILC.

Caritas-Switzerland has been our partner for over a decade now. The assistance they have given our program for working street children in Metro Manila and Negros complements our program with CDWs. The strategies we implement with the support from Caritas, particularly in Negros, forms a major part of the preventive aspect of our work.

Terre des hommes (TDH) has been our partner since 1997. It supports mainly the educational needs of CDW-beneficiaries, particularly in the cities of Davao and Bacolod. The TDH program also looks after the preventive aspect by providing emotional and material support to CDWs in the said cities. It also supports the research initiatives, as well as advocacy and awareness-raising activities of the Visayan Forum. It is now embarking on responding to the issue of trafficking of children.

Anti-Slavery International's (ASI) relationship with the Visayan Forum began in 1996. We were their principal partner in making a campaign video in 1999 to raise awareness about child domestic workers in the Philippines, which was shown widely in the Philippines and also to delegates of the ILC during the drafting of the ILO Convention 182. We also participated in a workshop organized by ASI in 1996, which led to the production of a handbook for research and action on CDWs.

Child Workers in Asia (CWA) is a network of NGOs working on children's issues in Asia. It publishes a newsletter, *Child Workers in Asia*, which has featured our experiences on child domestic work several times. It also lodges the Taskforce on CDW in Asia, composed of different NGOs working on this particular sector throughout Asia, of which the Visayan Forum is the convenor and lead agency.

As each of these actors contribute in its own way to the betterment of child domestic workers' circumstances, and the expansion of their options, it becomes even more important to look more deeply into the ambiguous situation of child domestic workers.

not quite family, not quite employee

their ambiguous role

O ur book began by highlighting the extent, magnitude, and worst forms of child domestic work. We have consequently called attention to the social, historical, cultural, economic, and legal context of the phenomenon, which brought us to a re-examination of the roles various institutions, agencies, organizations, and concerned citizens (both here and abroad) play in the life of a CDW. Let us now explore the latter's own role in her employer's household as well as her own family, starting with the ambiguity that characterizes her relationship with the employing household.

Many employers of domestic workers claim that their hired help is part of the family more than she is an employee. When Filipinos speak of family, we are liable to refer both to the nuclear family and the extended clan. As young kin, then, child domestic workers are supposed to be nurtured, assisted in their growth, and protected. For their part, children are expected to respond with gratitude, obedience, and loyalty. Some employers, though, have found that some domestic workers, as do relatives in any other capacity, tend to abuse the "family relationship". Ingratitude, disobedience, and treachery is sometimes the result of this "familiarity."

But are child domestic workers actually treated as part of the family?

If they are children of the family, then they would eat the same food as the employing household, even share the same mealtime. They would wear the same clothes as the other children of the household. They would go to the same school, and have the same time to study. They would sleep when the other children sleep, in a real bed in a private room, even though not their own, but probably with other children of their own sex. When they get sick, they would not be expected to work, but get the nurturing they need. The child domestic worker fortunate enough to be so privileged is an exception, not the rule.

Even when the child domestic is generally treated as part of the family, she is at the same time recognized as not being family. When it is time for the family to make

> Even when the child domestic is generally treated as part of the family, she is at the same time recognized as not being family. When it is time for the family to make certain decisions, she is not involved. This is the part of family life of which she cannot partake.

certain decisions, she is not involved. This is the part of family life of which she cannot partake.

If the child domestic worker is not treated as a member of the family, is she then treated as an employee?

If she is an employee, then there would be a contract. The contract would define, as contracts often do, the tasks and responsibilities of the child domestic worker. The amount of her wage and the manner of its payment, whether in cash or in kind, as well as frequency, would be delineated. The number of hours she is expected to work would be specified, including what holidays she can expect to receive. The proper way to terminate the employer-employee relationship would also be indicated. Just causes for deductions would be lined up, as well as other legitimate means of ensuring contract discipline.

> The CDW is called a member of the family, but is treated as a servant; she is working, working, always working, but only the employer knows the terms.

But how many domestic workers, much less child domestic workers, work under clear terms such as these? Verbal, unwritten agreement is the norm between an employer and a child domestic worker. This makes it impossible to prove the existence of any employment relationship, especially if the child is also the employer's kin.

The child domestic worker is called a member of the family, but is treated as a servant; she is working, working, always working, but only the employer knows the terms. These conflicting roles and the ambiguous treatment, naturally enough, confuses the child domestic worker, as well as the employing household.

The employer and the child are engaged in a constant guessing game as they try to figure out the rules of an ambiguous relationship.

Although CDWs are hired as substitutes for adult domestic workers, they are actually children. Although employers prefer to regard them as members of the family, they hired these children to work. Employers are generally unaware of the legal provisions that apply to domestic workers, to working children 18 years old and younger, as well as those that ban employing children below a certain age.

Why hire children for domestic work?

Employers of CDWs hire children mainly because they are available. Children are also accessible, affordable, easier to anage, more submissive, hard working, less complaining, and easier to train. Children come cheaper because they consume less resources than adults. They do not expect to obtain adult wages for the same work, since they recognize that they need more training. Thus, under the current law, unless their salary reaches PhP1,000 (US$20), they do not need social security benefits.

Many employers value the loyalty of their CDW, born of the child's gratitude for being taken into the household in the first place. CDWs pose less danger to the household's inhabitants, and are better companions for the employer's children. Employers expect them to behave as adults, even though they may be younger than some of the children they "play" with. This, combined with the fact that different employers have different ideas of the proper behavior of CDWs, compel the latter to adopt different personalities.

> The CDW performs multiple roles, or fulfills multiple needs, of the household: domestic servant, adopted child, playmate of the employer's children, and even business employee.

The CDW thus performs multiple roles, or fulfills multiple needs, of the household: domestic servant, adopted child, playmate of the employer's children, and even business employee. The combination changes with any given employer. When she changes employers, she has to learn a new set of expectations.

Aside from new expectations, child domestic workers often have to learn a new dialect. This is a common problem in a nation where even one region has as many as 11 dialects. Instructions can get jumbled: sometimes the same word has two different meanings in two different tongues. Mistakes are often regarded as the result of stupidity, instead of a language problem. To avoid further name-calling, a hapless child domestic claims to understand instructions even when she doesn't, which sometimes leads to additional problems.

Why do families allow the child to work as a domestic worker?

The families of child domestic workers live in underprivileged agricultural or fishing rural communities. Encouraging or allowing their children to work at such an early age is a survival mechanism of the poor rural Filipino family.

With expenditures of rural families increasing at a greater rate than their incomes, with the nation's richest families harvesting the lion's share of any increase in earnings, and an educational system unable to respond to the burgeoning needs of an increasingly younger population in a constantly modernizing world, sending one's own child to work in domestic service is a lesser evil than the few other options that exist.

Poor, rural families are compelled to make bitter decisions to survive. Many ask a daughter to put a brother's schooling before her own, since the boy will find a job more easily than she. Parents further believe that domestic labor can provide regular income. It brings in the much-needed cash, especially for an agricultural or fishing community devastated by natural calamity. There are entire households that have no recourse but to depend on one child domestic worker's income.

Parents regard their child's life as a domestic worker, especially in the city, as a far better option to life in rural poverty. Domestic service is perceived to guarantee the child food, clothing, shelter, and sometimes, education, which parents cannot provide her. Allowing or encouraging their child to work as a domestic worker hits two birds with one stone: the family has one less mouth to feed, and enjoys an additional source of income as well.

But why domestic work in particular? Parents prefer to place their children in domestic work for they see it as lighter and less arduous than other jobs available for children in their communities. It is better that the child works within the safety of a home than under the glare of the sun as a farmhand or fisher; or without it, as a miner; or in factories, the streets, and other dangerous places.

> Allowing or encouraging their child to work as a domestic worker hits two birds with one stone: the family has one less mouth to feed, and enjoys an additional source of income as well.

In addition, it is very easy to become a domestic worker. It requires neither formal training or schooling. One does not need a diploma or certificate to be hired. Everyone needs one, and many can afford it. The parent only needs to ask a friend, the child's godparent, a neighbor, the schoolteacher. More often than not, the employer-to-be is the one who has sent someone to scout the village for a domestic worker.

Also, the chance to work in the city raises the family's status in the community. Most parents are proud that their daughter is living and working in the big city. Domestic work is not how that daughter is supposed to spend the rest of her working life; it is just a stepping stone for better opportunities. Many parents, like their children, have many hopes riding on the possibilities offered by working in the city, for cash, with a benevolent employer.

When the hope is shattered, as it so often is, parents resort to fatalism. Even when a child domestic worker's complaint gets to court, parents prefer to settle it, being intimidated by the employer's superior financial standing. "The case will never prosper in court, anyway" is how they usually explain their actions.

This same fatalism marks many child domestic workers, who are profiled in the following chapter.

the dutiful child

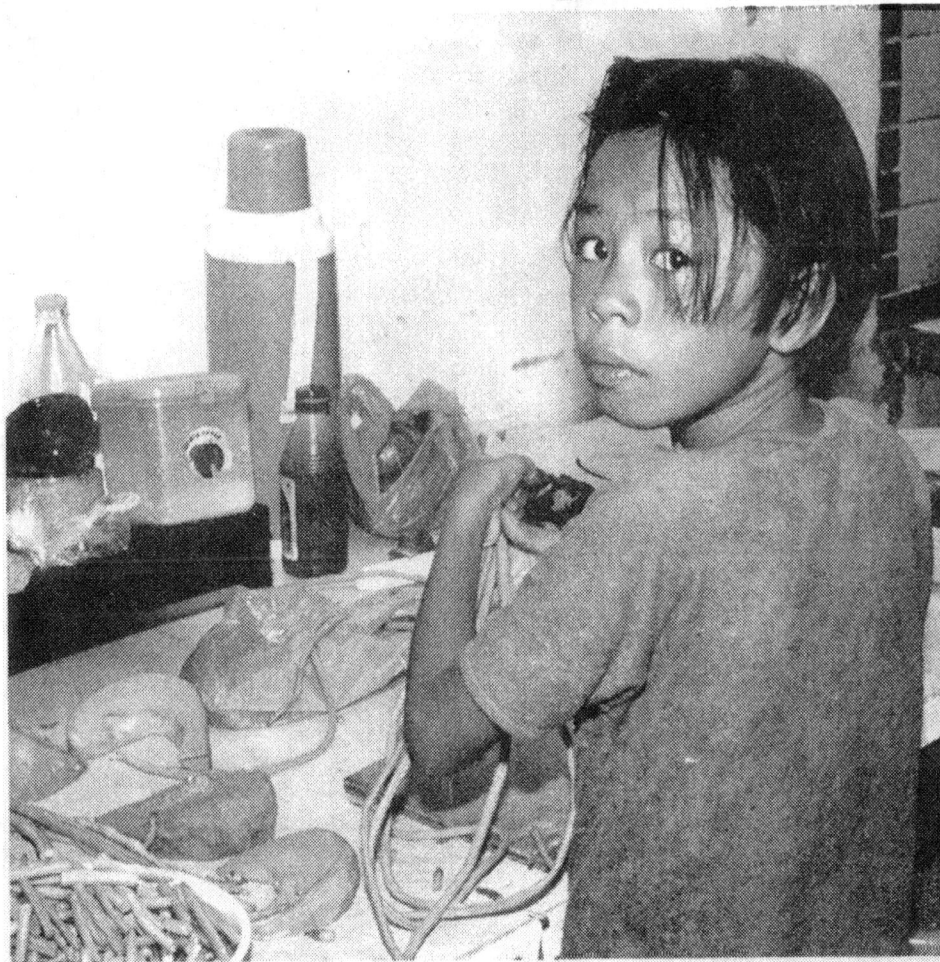

profile

Based on the database of child domestic workers served by the Visayan Forum since 1995, the typical child domestic worker is a single female, with high school education. She hails from a family involved in farming, farmworking, fishing, or informal sector activities in the Visayas. She is recruited by relatives, town mates or friends to engage in domestic work. She enters the world of work in order to help her family earn a living or to support herself. She has left her family and her hometown because of widespread poverty characterized by the pervasive lack of educational and livelihood opportunities. She is a migrant seeking greener pastures, hoping to pursue her studies while she works.

> ...the girl who enters domestic work takes on the responsibility of helping her family meet their basic human needs. She works both to help her family meet these needs, and at the same time relieve them of a burden: herself.

Socialized from early childhood to accept the concept of a "dutiful child", the girl who enters domestic work takes on the responsibility of helping her family meet their basic human needs. She works both to help her family meet these needs, and at the same time relieve them of a burden: herself. In many cases, she is working off her parents' debt to the employer. Many CDWs remit part or most of their income to support the schooling of a sibling, more often than not, a brother.

Some child domestic workers begin their career by working for their schoolteacher or a neighbor in their own village at the age of 8. They move on to another employer, who lives in town. From there, they usually go to the city to find the same work. From the city in their own region, they then proceed to their region's growth center, and finally, to Manila.

For many, working in somebody else's home, especially their relatives, may be their only passport to a better life. It may be a second chance to have a good home, perhaps an opportunity to complete elementary education at least. It may be a haven from an abusive parent. It is the chance for regular meals, perhaps the opportunity to save for next semester's tuition fees, while the farm their parents till is stricken by drought or by civil strife.

The typical domestic worker has no social security. Days off work are limited, if at all provided. She has to budget the salary she receives to cover not only her personal supplies, but remittances as well. She often finds her employer as too demanding or too strict. She endures verbal abuse, while receiving low wages for an excessive workload that extends to duties outside the employing household.

In our experience, seldom do we see a sociable, expressive, articulate, and confident child domestic worker.

A lot of CDWs are distant relatives of some employers, dependent on the employer for food and shelter. It is very difficult for them to demand a few hours each week for their studies. Most of them believe that work and school are interdependent: it is not an "either-or" option. Schooling is desirable, but work is a necessity. Combining work and school fulfils both the need to survive and to prepare for a competitive adult life.

Many find it difficult to study even when their employer does give them the time they need. On one hand, it is indeed harder to concentrate when one is tired. On the other hand, most CDWs do not display a great deal of creativity and imagination. These qualities are indeed desirable for students, but they have no room in the CDW's world. It is the employer's creativity and imagination they must obey, often stifling their own.

The dutiful child grows into the dutiful child domestic worker: a little adult. Some child domestics, even though they are being treated unfairly, think twice about leaving.

In adapting to the different whims of the individuals in the same employing household, not to mention a new household when they change employers, they learn very early the appropriate responses to each member of their employing household. In so doing, they learn to curb their own responses. They are thus not as expressive as other children of their own age. Many are shy of socializing with others, especially with those who display authoritative characteristics or are financially well off.

Their deafening silence, vigilant hesitation and distrust of other people indicate trauma. The dutiful child with dreams, who began a journey of hope, withers into the retiring, inhibited, silent, and hesitant adult-in-a-child's-body who doesn't dare to dream.

> The dutiful child with dreams, who began a journey of hope, withers into the retiring, inhibited, silent, and hesitant adult-in-a-child's-body who doesn't dare to dream.

Their stories, and the way they tell them, suggest that they do not consider most incidents of verbal and physical abuse as violence, but only as an "occupational hazard." They do nothing about it. They accept it as their lot in life. Abuse happens so often to so many child domestics and domestic workers in general that it is regarded as a normal part of the job. They rarely seek justice for the crimes committed against them. Their attitude of unquestioning acceptance calms them. This attitude is frequently used to justify not taking any legal action against an employer's abuses. Only sexual and religious abuse are seen as requiring action, usually in the form of leaving their employer.

> Abuse happens so often to so many child domestics and domestic workers in general that it is regarded as a normal part of the job. They rarely seek justice for the crimes committed against them.

Even when they are unfairly accused of theft, many prefer to just pay the amount back either through work or in cash. Employers easily intimidate domestic workers, none so easily as children. Many have been jailed on the strength of an employer's accusation alone. This is a lamentably common form of retaliation by employers; sometimes it is an attempt to divert attention from the abuses they perpetuate. The victim becomes the perpetrator, the abuser the accuser. In these ironic twists, many domestics become fatalistic.

Strong fatalism is a natural response to the abuses they suffer. At the Visayan Forum, we found it difficult to extract their personal opinions. They would always say, "That's the way things are."

Their experience of total dependence on their employers breeds shyness and awe, and obstructs litigation. Having a humane employer is considered good luck: an exception, not the general rule. In their experience, the general rule is having an employer who abuses them.

Child domestic workers, because of their working conditions and the hazards that come with it, most importantly because they have little or no outside support, tend to develop psychosocial trauma due to constant abuse. Their intellectual, emotional and physical development is stunted. Their self-esteem is severely reduced. Due to the conflict between their being children and their role as premature adults, many child domestics suffer an identity crisis.

It is this dutiful child-adult who instills urgency in our goal to reduce the exploitation of children, and combat abuses against them.

But it is the child with dreams whom we try to reach in our work at the Visayan Forum. But, as the following chapter will show, after five years of working with them, we feel that we have barely begun.

case story: Rosario

At the age of 9, Rosario started working as a household helper with her hometown's teacher so that she could enroll in first grade. After 4 months, she left her employer because she was blamed for the loss of the carabao. She went to a remote barrio to continue schooling until second grade, even though she often had to go without food. When she was 12 years old, in third grade, she worked with a family whose father was an elementary school teacher of her elder sister. There she stayed for 3 years up to the time she finished fifth grade.

She went to Davao City at the age of 14 to look for work and to continue schooling. She only lasted 3 months before going home. She then left again for General Santos City to look for other work. There, she landed in the wax factory where she and 11 others cooked and repacked floor wax. She was paid PhP500 (US$10) for working from 6 in the morning to 8 in the evening, sleeping on the cement floor where they worked, shielded only by sackcloth, and eating only what was left by the Chinese owners. An incident prompted them to escape: Rosario was blamed for the loss of 4 big boxes of wax. Since no one admitted the loss, all of them where locked up at the workplace for 5 days with no light except for what came through a very small window near the attic. They managed to break the small window one evening and escaped through there.

She went back to Davao City in January 1998, looking for employment. She was introduced to the *Kasambahay* Program by her employer.

part 3

strategies

"Putting first and foremost
their best interests
as children..."

what works for filipino CDWs?

development of the visayan forum's approaches

When we began, we set up the services at our office, and waited for the child domestic worker's call or visit. After a few months and a bare trickle of cases, we realized that we had to go out ourselves and find them. This gave us our first hint that these children were isolated from mainstream society.

We sought to find them in their workplace — their employer's home — the classic organizing approach for workers. This proved little better than the "walk-in" method: going door-to-door in posh subdivisions looking for child domestic workers was, in a word, counter-productive. The more we sought them, the less the likelihood of finding any. These difficulties began to teach us about their situation.

Even those we did manage to contact in this manner could not speak freely about their situation: could they trust us? Would they offend the employer who was right there with us, or at least within hearing distance? It is very difficult for these children, disciplined as they are to speak only when spoken to, taught as they are not to complain, socialized as they are into accepting abuse as part of the job, inculcated as they are with fatalism, to open up to us quickly — no matter how sympathetic we appear to be. They taught us about themselves, even as they could not articulate these feelings outright.

Accepting these lessons, we sought for other ways to reach them. Since reaching them at their workplace was out of the question, where else could we find them?

We found them in schools, often with their charges in tow, some as students themselves. We found them in church, going to mass or availing of temporary shelter. We found them in novitiates, which took them in during their period of crisis. Finally, we found them where they were most numerous: at public parks, on their day off. Here, unconfined by the four walls of a house, at very little cost, in the midst of hundreds of people who do not give them orders — here, they relax. Here, they meet their town mates, relatives, and friends. We have found this to be true not only in Manila, but in other regions as well.

> It is very difficult for these children, disciplined as they are to speak only when spoken to, taught as they are not to complain, socialized as they are into accepting abuse as part of the job, inculcated as they are with fatalism, to open up to us quickly — no matter how sympathetic we appear to be. They taught us about themselves, even as they could not articulate these feelings outright.

Thus we focused on finding them at the parks and other recreational places, churches, and schools. We introduced ourselves, and found that many did not have all Sundays off: we made the Sunday-at-the-Park a regular activity, so that they can find us there whenever they are free. Often, they did not have the entire day off: we soon realized that we had to be able to conduct activities in three hours only, four at most. Since they were tired from their work, we had to be able to grab and retain their attention: our activities must thus be visually engaging and participatory. Disinclined as they were to trust strangers, it often took co-child domestic workers to convince them to participate: soon, these children were inviting other children to come along and meet us.

We discussed their rights, using flipcharts and flyers; we talked with them about their problems and their goals. We encouraged them to meet other child domestic workers, and to play. We saw them blossom: from being wary and unsure, they developed confidence and assurance. We realized that, with appropriate training, they could become leaders of their own ranks; facilitate counseling, discussions, and data collection; and provide a strong peer support system for their fellow child domestic workers.

Our journey in the world of child domestic work entailed not only cataloguing what we have witnessed, but more importantly, reflecting on what we have done to better their lot. What have we in the Visayan Forum done thus far to improve the world of child domestic workers?

We have barely begun. As we write down our lived experiences and interactions with Filipino child domestic workers, we recognize the complexity of the phenomenon, which requires an array of responses. The dearth in documented programs of other institutions made us more reflective, as our initial actions in the field evolved into well-entrenched strategies.

These strategies should be seen as part of a broader approach of helping society redefine the institutions of the family, work, and school, among others. Are these

> We have barely begun. As we write down our lived experiences and interactions with Filipino child domestic workers, we recognize the complexity of the phenomenon, which requires an array of responses.

effective at the personal, community, institutional and societal levels?

Let us take a snapshot of the past two years.

We reached 5,216 child domestic workers in the field alone. Of these, 47 percent were contacted in schools where they were mostly studying (82 percent), while some were waiting for their wards (18 percent). The parks yielded 44 percent; other agencies or institutions referred 8 percent; 1 percent walked in.

We counseled 1,654 children either directly or one-on-one, by telephone, by letter, by peers, and by visits to their workplace.

Many ran away from abusive employers. Our center catered to 278 children needing a temporary place to stay in while awaiting referral to other agencies and, whenever the child and her family agreed, reintegration with her family.

Almost every week, we assisted child domestic workers in obtaining medication and hospital care, and referred them to clinics or other medical institutions for consultation or check-up. There were 264 patients in all.

We aided 133 children who sought legal advice and solutions. With our partners in government and civil society, these children tasted the power of the law to dispense justice against the abuses they experienced. Our assistance included facilitating claims on unpaid wages, going with them to hearings, making affidavits and/or counter-affidavits, arranging bail, facilitating out-of-court settlements, providing lawyers, and referring them to legal and paralegal institutions.

In six schools all over the archipelago, we conducted field outreach activities because many child domestic workers were involved in their alternative education program. We helped increase the survival rate by at least 20 percent.

As many as 2,410 child domestic workers became aware of their rights and entitlements, whom to contact in case of emergency, and how to survive the initial impact of abuses through unconventional training and orientation methods.

Some 116 child domestic worker leaders advanced to more serious trainings exploring leadership, team building, organizing, counseling, and self-development.

They championed the first-ever nationwide network of CDW organizations, which took off early in 1996. SUMAPI *(Samahan at Ugnayan ng mga Manggagawang Pantahanan sa Pilipinas*, roughly translated as Association and Linkage of Domestic Workers in the Philippines) means "to join." They overcame their scatteredness and invisibility to build SUMAPI into a vibrant organization of 5,000 members in 17 core groups.

Around 8,000 domestic workers regularly participate in park (4,000), port (1,000) and school (3,000 in 7 alternative schools) outreach activities nationwide through this organization.

As a parent organization, the Visayan Forum is proud of SUMAPI. Since its inception, SUMAPI has been a potent vehicle for raising public awareness and serving as a catchment mechanism for members in distress.

> Since its inception, SUMAPI has been a potent vehicle for raising public awareness and serving as a catchment mechanism for members in distress.

Some 15 members compose the experienced speakers' pool that has set foot in the most dusty rural town halls and the most elegant palaces worldwide. They have testified in front of policemen, legislators, presidents, kings and world leaders.

Although they were told everyday that domestic work was all they could ever hope to do with any degree of competency, many SUMAPI members grew into humane, effective and persuasive activists for their own ranks. They watch over each other. Through their ever-growing network of cooperative employers, town mates, friends and relatives, they identify, trace and reach even severely isolated domestic workers.

They spot, report, and monitor child domestic workers suffering from abuse and other difficulties. They negotiate with employers of child domestic workers. Using a flipchart, they inform CDWs of their rights, and help the latter see and value their contribution to society. They facilitate child domestic workers' access to available services.

As a group, they help each other find hope in the face of despair, laughter amid pain, inner strength against coercive environments — in short, resiliency.

Finally, all these gains — as well as the failures along the way due to factors we slowly began to recognize — led us to think harder about sustaining our efforts.

Towards sustainability, the program has successfully enrolled more than 500 domestic workers in the Social Security System as of this writing.

A sustained media advocacy for the past three years has put the issue of domestic work into national consciousness. More people are now using *kasambahay* or household partner to ascribe a positive social image to these silent workers.

The staff has dialogued with more than 1,000 employers of the SUMAPI members to reinforce good practices. National television programs and print media outlets have started to help in this process of social retrospection, and by virtue of their reach alone, millions of employers have expanded their consciousness about the rights of domestic workers.

More than a hundred teachers in *Kasambahay*-organized classrooms have also volunteered to help in the efforts, being the second parents of these child domestic workers.

In aid of legislation, some 40 legislators are co-authors of a landmark Magna Carta dubbed as *Batas Kasambahay*. Various sectors from civil society groups, law enforcement, justice system, government, the academe, and people's organizations have also thrown their support behind the law and its enabling principles.

We consider all we have accomplished as only the beginning of a profound change in society. We feel we have merely conceived and given birth to the forces that will usher in that change. We hope you join us in making this change possible, by learning from our lessons.

learning while living

synthesis of the visayan forum
strategies

The preceding chapter gave us some idea of the range of activities needed to operationalize certain strategies. Here, we offer you our actual experiences in implementing a program for child domestic workers.

While the following discussions of the Visayan Forum's strategies also come from the perspectives of employers, legislators, parents, government workers, and other NGO workers, we will do our best to incorporate many of the concerns raised by the child domestic workers themselves. We are rather overwhelmed by the complexity of their perceptions, because different victims behave differently in different circumstances. This may be due to varying levels of resiliency and awareness of each child domestic worker, and perhaps due as well to our own biases in perceiving their reality.

We hope that this will not obstruct our efforts towards a genuine reflection. We hope that these may be viewed as a continuing contribution to the search for better solutions and more effective approaches.

This is a reflexive synthesis because we try to theorize from our experience. In the absence of sufficient empirical data that are important in any attempt to systematize any body of knowledge, we believe we can still come up with generalizations that others may still question on the grounds of applicability. The term "reflexive" is often used in sociological work, denoting "self-correction." It aptly describes many of the fine-tunings and even "knee-jerk" reactions during implementation, caused by the fact that we had neither prior experience nor knowledge to bank on. It is a particular form of reflection based on immediate experience, characterized by raw learning, with the chances for success equal to the risks of failure. Some call it learning by doing: for us, it has become learning by living.

Different countries, each with its own socio-political, cultural and economic context, may find that defining what works for domestic workers will always be subject to debate and, perhaps, pessimism. In this light, we hope that our efforts to network with other groups, aside from hosting national and international conferences on the issue, will benefit all who wish to serve the interests of child domestic workers.

We offer our systematized documentation and analysis of our field experiences that others may start with a fine-tuned model in the future.

sustainability principles

1 Put first and foremost their best interests as children: treat them first as children and secondly as workers.

2 Put in place a national network of institutions with special facilities for abused and runaway domestic workers.

3 Promote free, accessible, and quality education for CDWs, and making it relevant to their special needs as working children.

4 Make the invisible visible.

5 Improve employer-employee relationship is central to any analysis and intervention for any child domestic worker.

6 Reaffirm the right to decent work and recognize that CDWs are in fact productive members of society.

7 Constantly improve domestic workers' productivity requires more attention than it received in the past.

8 Work for a blanket ban on child domestic work for those below 15 years.

not necessarily a welfare approach

direct services

Despite the recent increase in national attention on CDWs in the Philippines, they remain the most neglected group of abused children. They are on their own, having few lifelines to cling to except their employers' benevolence. It is difficult for them to contact friends, who may themselves be burdened with problems at work. These are the workers who, because of their isolation, seldom attempt to break out of abusive situations. Any delay in responding to their call for help can spell the difference between hope and despair, freedom and indefinite bondage, or even between life and death.

Recognizing that providing direct services is welfare-directed, the gravity of abuses dealt with everyday requires us to set up an integrated, holistic and proactive facilitation of social services. This stems from our belief that we should put the best interests of children first and foremost. Ultimately, we want assisted CDWs to become part of the expanding social network of child domestic workers within or outside SUMAPI. In this way, they can focus on other areas of self-development.

Direct services include, but are not limited to, providing emotional and material support such as medical, para-legal, telephone hotline counseling, educational support, crisis intervention, and temporary shelter. These are offered in centers, workplaces, schools, and even in recreational parks. These must be based on where and when the child domestic worker is immediately available, because time for contact is very limited. It is more difficult to undo damage to the child if we allow delays in getting her out of abusive situations. A child in danger cannot wait.

Recently, the Visayan Forum included registering domestic workers with the Social Security System as part of its direct services. Many CDWs are not aware that law mandates employers to enlist them and shoulder part of the contributions. Access to social security solves many of the problems emanating from the employer-employee relationship. In case of work-related illnesses and accidents, CDWs currently pay for their own medication and hospitalization, or have the expenses deducted from salaries. By registering, they can also make salary advances and loans that they can remit home, to finance burial and other needs brought about by calamities affecting the family.

Sustainability Principle 1

Put first and foremost their best interests as children: treat them first as children and secondly as workers.

In all actions concerning children, the best interests of the child shall take primary consideration. A basic principle, this is best understood in the context of children's development. We should treat them first as children and secondly as workers, although for many of them, the roles may swiftly shift in order for them to survive.

To ensure the best interest of the child, it is therefore important to note the three ideals of child-centered approaches:

1. Put the child's safety/security first, over and above output, or other interests.

2. Understand the child domestic worker's situation from her own standpoint. This may be done through participatory research, direct interaction, seeking solutions together with her, and involving as many members of her support network as possible.

3. Make child development a priority through psychosocial interventions geared to enhance resiliency, including influencing the external conditions that affect her individual capacities.

4. Expand the participation of child domestic workers by organizing and involving them in advocacy activities, in cognizance of both their capacities and limitations.

Providing loans through the SSS is one sure way for government to share the burden, arm-in-arm with employers and CDWs alike.

Enrolling child domestic workers in the SSS is a continuing effort. But there are other effective ways that make social security accessible on a massive scale. The high profile Domestic Workers' Day and continuous monthly registration in parks are among them. These efforts are also good venues to document profiles, introduce the use of work contracts, and advise employers of the legal provisions pertaining to the employment of domestic workers.

There is no doubt that existing organizations have the capacity to provide these types of direct services for child domestic workers. However, the lack of focus for this specific group of children may limit the social impact of these services. This work requires special attention and understanding of the issues characteristic of child domestic workers.

Sustainability Principle 2

Put in place a national network of institutions with special facilities for abused and runaway domestic workers.

Today, the number of institutions working with street children is far more than those working with abused young maids. Yet if we think about it, there are as many child domestic workers as there are children working in the streets. The abuses inflicted on CDWs are equally dehumanizing, albeit more invisible. Their situation is also comparable to the plight of prostituted children.

It is high time we focus equal national attention on child domestic workers. Considering the lack of alternatives for abused CDWs, they can easily slide into prostitution and street vagrancy. The Visayan Forum has documented many such cases.

"But we can always accommodate abused maids using our existing resources," institutions may say. The truth is, they do.

It is also true, however, that they do not usually cover the many aspects of the abused child domestic worker's needs. More is required than simply mixing them with other types of children. Child domestic workers are generally less expressive and less comfortable in a group. Suffering in bondage has very deep repercussions on their sociability.

They would rather confide in a fellow domestic worker. Empathy is very important, and thus should be gained first.

Most of them are unlike street children who can be very voluble and articulate when they want our attention.

This is not to discriminate against street children. But the Visayan Forum's experience in two different programs under the same roof, for both types of children, eventually boiled down to separating activities and staff responsible for them.

There are further practical reasons for separate programs for child domestic workers. First, it may take a very long time to return abused child domestic workers to their families because the latter have to be contacted in remote locations in the countryside. It may even take longer for them to come to the center, because of financial reasons. In this light, setting up regional offices such as Davao, Bacolod and Batangas has been very practical.

Second, there are very few hotlines, and these are not commonly known. The Visayan Forum has only five working lines nationwide, and they are not even enough to accommodate the volume of callers. Developing a nationwide hotline network can widen the efforts to reach behind closed doors.

Third, most victims of child trafficking are lured to work as domestic workers. This is the recruiter's easiest selling point to parents and children. Since trafficking involves an intricate nationwide network, there should also be an intricate network of organizations and government agencies providing, in total, a holistic and organized set of interventions.

Indeed, many institutions are needed to offer help to CDWs. Ultimately, these should engage in creative synergy to share resources, expertise and databases, to become an effective catchment and support network of these invisible children.

There are special concerns when providing direct services to abused child domestic workers. One particularity is that it is best to make it programmatic with the other strategies, especially at the start. For example, we combine research and immediate action on the problems they reveal. It often requires a series of interactions for us to win their trust. Only then do most child domestic workers begin to confide their deeper problems. Only then will deeper levels of approach be possible.

We call this a "layered" approach. Using intake sheets, the Visayan Forum volunteers first record individual details of newly-reached CDWs so that they can follow them up by telephone or written correspondence. This may seem an obvious thing to do, but it becomes handy especially when we may meet a child domestic worker only once or twice a month, or perhaps never again. We cannot interview her just anytime. We have to wait for each opportunity when she becomes available.

About two thirds of the cases the Visayan Forum has handled are harvested using this programmatic approach. The rest are from other institutions and hotline outlets that do not have specific services for these child domestic workers, whom they then refer to us. As of this writing, the number of minors illegally recruited for domestic work that we intercepted in ports of entry is also increasing.

Going deeper into the particularities of delivering direct services to child domestic workers, we found some unique aspects of several processes, namely: investigation, mediation, removal, pursuing legal action, and healing, recovery, and reintegration.

Investigation

When a person reports an abuse, it is crucial to recognize that he/she made a difficult decision. He/She may be the victim, a neighbor, or a concerned citizen who put his/her life on the line. In the case of a hotline report, the caller may not call again if we fail to make him/her feel safe because he/she may feel that we do not recognize the urgency and gravity of the situation.

Upon receiving the report and processing the information, we have to decide immediately whether to investigate or not, and more especially how and when. Immediate action is sometimes impossible because the address given is difficult to find; employers are not around (there are situations where child domestic workers are only able to call telephone hotlines when the employer is asleep or away from home for a long period of time), or we decide to try and invite the child's parents to join us during the negotiation.

When we enter a house, we must be very careful not to inadvertently worsen the situation. Employers naturally feel that their integrity is being challenged or put at risk in this scenario. It is important to make them understand that we are not there to judge, but only to verify a report.

Investigation is very tricky. We must always assume that we do not have all the solid facts. Yet we must take the risk, which may also be our only chance to help the child domestic worker. If we fail to pull her out, there is a distinct probability that her employer will castigate her after we have left. Rather than have that happen, it would have been better not to investigate in the first place.

This is what happened on our first major attempt at removal. The case involved six children, most of whom had acute respiratory illnesses by that time. The employer agreed to release only five. One — who turned out to be the most abused and the most intimidated — decided to stay behind. She was warned not to jump ship. A year later, we found out that after we left, she was severely beaten and locked up.

BASIC PROCESSES

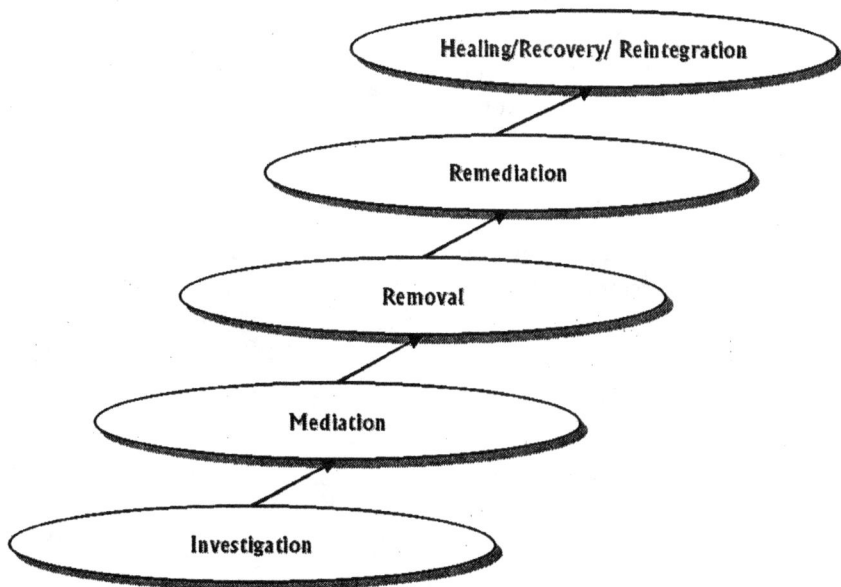

Healing/Recovery/ Reintegration

Remediation

Removal

Mediation

Investigation

A very pro-active and non-confrontational way of investigation is to strike a deal with organized employers. This allows us to visit their child domestic workers regularly. This is easier done in small urban centers like Batangas, where the influence of the Church is very dominant.

Mediation

This is another complex process. We should always strive for a win-win situation. The aim is to strike a balance between the best interests of the child and that of the employer. While we may ultimately retrieve the child in distress, we must take care not to push employers to the wall.

They need to feel that they at least have some neutral ground, a comfort zone. A feeling of fairness to both parties is enhanced with the presence of neutral actors such as a respected priest, a licensed social worker, a known teacher. Police need not enter the picture: they can calmly stay outside the house premises, ready to respond should matters get out of control.

Mediation is difficult for NGOs like the Visayan Forum because we are not mandated to conduct such methods of inspection, as a labor inspector normally can in a factory. It pays to be cordial, not antagonistic, because antagonism can create more problems than already exist.

Removal

The drama of mediation usually concludes in removing the child, although this is not its primary end goal. Removing a child should never become an end in itself, nor exposed as the juicy subject of media hype. The calmer the process, the safer the child.

When do we remove a child? The answer to this question may appear to be very elementary, but based on experience, certain rules of thumb must be observed.

One, we should have clear alternatives for the child as part of the plan of action after removal.

Second, removal is easier when prior contact and arrangements with the child's family members have been taken care of. Parents and relatives are in a better position to invoke their custodial rights when negotiating with abusive employers. Employers tend to resist the custodial rights of the child, which may prolong the agony of the child awaiting release. This is the main reason why the Visayan Forum supports the granting of third party rights through legislation as embodied in the Magna Carta.

Third, we should ensure that employers are allowed to check, in the presence of a third party, all the belongings the child domestic worker takes with her before leaving. There have been many cases in the past where child domestic workers, even with the most valid reasons for leaving, end up being charged with petty theft or are jailed. This is a common means of employer retaliation, sometimes also done to prevent the victim from taking legal action first. The abused then becomes the guilty party.

Remediation

The Visayan Forum seriously considers taking legal action to punish perpetuators. The hardest cases are murder, rape and physical torture. We recognize legal action as one of the ways to redress grievances as part of the healing process of the child and her family.

While this is the next logical step after removing a child from an exploitative situation, it need not be the only recourse. Many CDWs prefer to just set aside the harrowing experiences and look forward to the future. Others get intimidated by the superior financial and social standing of employers, and feel that corresponding legal penalties are not commensurate to the time, effort and money they need to invest in legal battles.

It is also hard to reconstruct a truly factual testimony that can stand in court. Such accounts are easily demolished by the employer's own testimony. After all, the latter can produce collaborative testimonies of other witnesses who are part of the household. The child has only her own testimony. It comes down to the word of the child versus the word of the employer. What happens when the accused employer is a socially respected leader in the community?

For these reasons, the most common para-legal action is a proper accounting of delayed or unpaid wages. Many child domestic workers consider this a more achievable form of justice. It may also be the only means to scrape together the fare she needs to return to the province. The absence of impermeable laws against recruitment agencies is also a loophole that we must look into.

Healing, recovery and reintegration

Ideally, this should happen under the roof of the parents' protective home. If we should find parents to be incapacitated, long-term care by adoptive institutions is an option. This is a long process, and NGOs with limited resources can only provide short-term help contributive to this long-term goal.

The Visayan Forum offers temporary shelter as immediately needed by victims. It may be necessary only until the child is able to make a responsible decision, an informed choice, among the options available to her. These options can be as simple as going home, going back to school, pursuing legal action, and/or finding another job. Whatever option she may take, she must be involved in many stages, and feel responsible for her own actions.

Abused child domestic workers commonly want to find another employer. The Visayan Forum does not discount this option when the other alternatives are not immediately viable. By this time, processing their experiences towards a more resilient view of life is a must. While the Visayan Forum does not see itself as a placement agency, practicality sometimes necessitates finding the child a job.

from commodity to empowerment tool

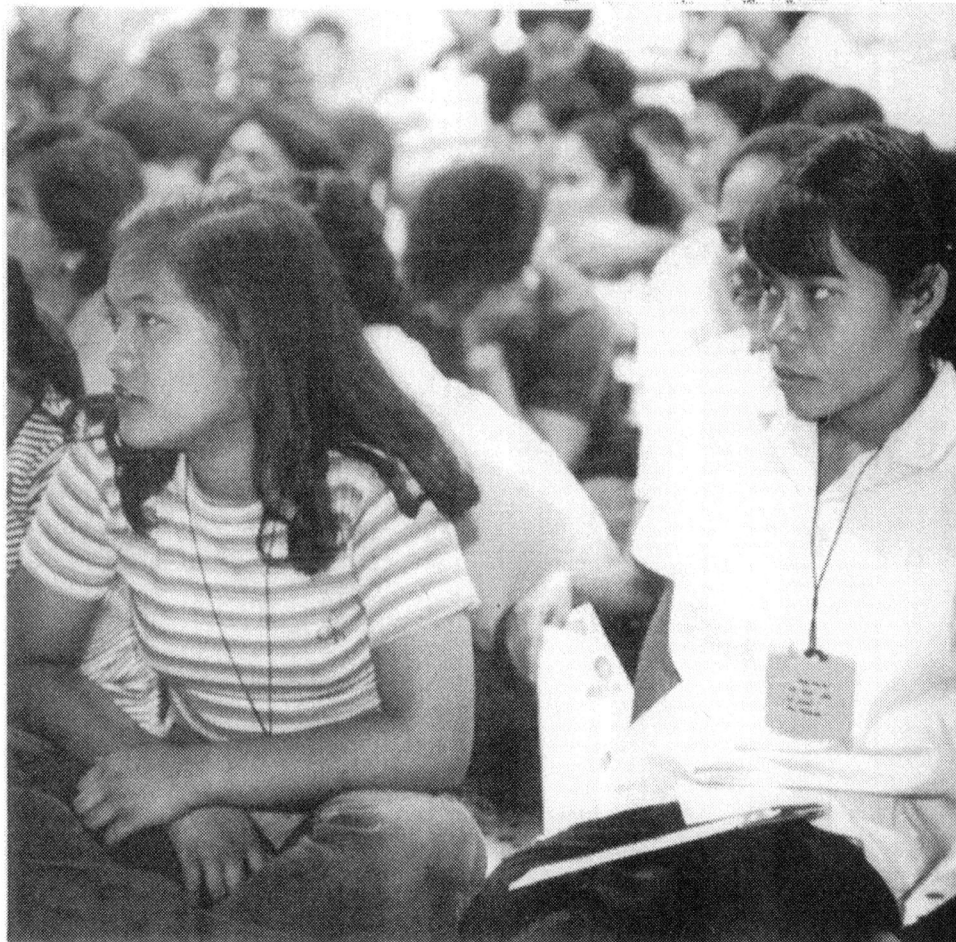

education

Providing opportunities and expanding the context for education is a core strategy for child domestic workers. The strategy also recognizes the existence of many alternative education schemes in the country. These include distance education, special night classes, Sunday school programs, and short-term skills training courses.

Setting up similar programs was therefore not a priority strategy of the *Kasambahay* Program. Establishing an expensive training center is not a sound economic strategy because many institutions are already under-utilized in the first place.

Instead, the project built on the existence of such structures. Since 1997, the Visayan Forum has been reaching out to CDWs in both public and private secondary schools as an integral part of expanding the network of SUMAPI. The initial approach was to maintain selected deserving child domestic worker students by providing them with a fixed amount of yearly scholarship.

...helping CDWs attain a harmonious balance between work and school contributes more to their development.

This traditional approach of scholarship education, while it had its successes, was not always truly effective. It helped only a few, mostly the initial members of SUMAPI. It also failed to take into account the fact that individual child domestic workers required different levels and forms of assistance incongruent with the fixed regular stipends. The approach was also an unwitting form of dole-out strategy, curtailing the initiatives of child domestic workers to explore other ways of bridging their financial needs.

Most importantly, we realized later that helping CDWs attain a harmonious balance between work and school contributes more to their development.

Child domestic workers do not always perceive working and studying as mutually exclusive. One is not an alternative life choice which excludes the other. The ideal, of course, is for the child's family to be able to afford to send her to school within their own locality, in the province. But once under the guardianship of an employer, a CDW away from home faces the reality that, when allowed, she is both a worker and a student.

Schooling is desirable, and work is a necessity. The combination of both offers a concrete practical solution for survival and development towards a competitive adult life. This social reality can, of course, be changed if government increases its capacity to provide free education for all children.

We also realized that for most child domestic workers, the school is their second home. Teachers are their second parents. It is a place to make friends, for recreation, for socialization. Meeting classmates regularly provides them with development opportunities beyond closed doors. The Visayan Forum therefore fine-tuned its approach by combining the following strategies:

- Providing emergency educational support to prevent CDWs from dropping out because they are unable to pay for their tuition. We pay the school directly upon the recommendation of the teacher, the principal and the local officer of the domestic workers' organization.

- Engaging in technical cooperation with the school administration, which led to the adjustment of the school curriculum. Since then, teachers have allotted an hour a week incorporating the teaching of domestic worker's rights, life skills, and the like. The teachers also agreed to schedule a retreat seminar for each class each year to process the work and family experiences of the children.

- Conducting training and awareness orientation for teachers about the plight of domestic workers, their role as caregivers, and how to refer suspected cases of abuse. In effect, the teachers have become our allies.

- Intervening on behalf of domestic workers whenever they have problems with their employers to head off any possible interruption of their academic life.

□ Scheduling group orientations of employers, in cooperation with the school officials, to improve employer-employee relationship which is crucial to the child's performance in school.

□ Giving tutorials, often needed when they return to the school regime for the first time after a lengthy absence.

□ Organizing each class as sub-groups of the domestic workers' association allowed us to coordinate activities like training and field trips, among others. This also helped us monitor the performance of each working child better and faster. In addition, this served as the children's immediate peer support system, which sustains an individual's determination to study when the combined demands of work and studying seem to be excessive.

□ Supporting the setting up of Activity Centers by and for SUMAPI members. This physical lounge is an important venue for all the services and strategies initiated by the Visayan Forum, together with teachers and other students.

There are problems attendant to combining work and school. Aside from the inherent difficulties of combining work and school such as heavy workloads, inability to pay tuition fees, and chronic absenteeism, other trends were also observed.

Employers tend to decrease child domestic workers' salaries, or not pay them at all, in exchange for providing transportation allowances. A child domestic worker receiving PhP800 (US$16) a month may only receive half because her employer now gives PhP100 (US$2) per weekend, for example.

Child domestic workers are expected to perform the same workload by adjusting the time schedule. Instead of ironing clothes in the afternoon, for example, they finish the job late in the evening after coming from class.

Some employers make the choice of working and studying mutually exclusive. They prefer having full-time servants at home. Many CDWs are apprehensive of asking permission to study, for fear of losing their jobs.

Many child domestic workers who were not able to study under their previous employer find these adjustments justifiable. Thus, rather than risk letting the opportunity to study vanish before their very eyes, they agree to these arrangements, taking on both roles as workers and as students.

Sustainability Principle 3

Promote free, accessible, and quality education for CDWs, and making it relevant to their special needs as working children.

In the situation where education is not free, our efforts should focus on helping child domestic workers access existing alternative educational schemes. We can take further steps in strengthening and enhancing these "second homes" by injecting flexible, innovative and proactive support approaches that can ultimately be institutionalized with the creative cooperation between teachers, CDW students, and employers.

Institutionalizing the *Kasambahay* Program in these schools requires not only redefining the school's vision, mission, goals and strategies so that these help instead of hinder child domestic workers. It also involves organizing group structures (such as SUMAPI); regularizing activities for child domestic workers, teachers and employers; and setting up physical structures (such as Activity Centers).

case story: Rosalinda

Rosalinda worked for 11 employers just to be able to go to school. She was employed as a domestic worker as early as 9 years old. Her anguish and pains through these years corrupted her childhood.

When she was 12, she was nearly raped by a 70-year-old man, the father of her employer, who tried to win her with money and food. After leaving her former employer, she moved to work in another household where she slept at the nipa shack located outside the main house. In this household, she was fed with leftover foods; her work entailed doing all the household chores by herself. She also went through the ordeal of being hit, her hair pulled, and even slapped, not only by her employer but by other members of the household. Her duties included carrying feeds uphill where the pig sty was situated. One of her former employers paid her PhP1 (US$.02) a day, and at times none.

Because of her fervent desire to finish her education, she attended night school. After doing back-breaking work during the day, she walks to school daily, and returns home exhausted, facing still another load of household chores that needs to be done. Once, she came home at 6:30 pm because they had some practice in school. However, her employer was unmindful of her excuse. Rosalinda was locked out of the house until dawn.

Now that she is shielded from relentless employers, she helps the Visayan Forum advocate for the rights of CDWs.

planting seeds of their freedom

organizing the SUMAPI

The absence or limited awareness and understanding among child domestic workers of their basic rights remains a key empowerment issue. This curtails the sustainability of other strategies — be it direct service, education, advocacy or networking.

It is in this light that organizations of domestic workers, as in the case of SUMAPI, are important channels for advocacy and for provision of safety mechanisms against abuses within their own ranks. Without organized action among domestic workers, individual empowerment will not be sustained on a massive scale.

"We give a human face to an invisible, lowly regarded sector"

"We give a human face to an invisible, lowly regarded sector," says Maribel Pantajo, 16, now SUMAPI President, who started to work at the age of 13. Constant physical and verbal abuse by her employer and her ward forced her to seek assistance through a telephone hotline network.

For migrant domestic workers who are confined to endless chores for endless days, always on call to perform services to satisfy their employers' personal needs, being a part of SUMAPI finally gives them back their voice. At times, television networks cover SUMAPI rallies and other policy advocacy actions. Members are invited as guests in radio programs. They participate in strategic planning sessions of various child labor networks in the country.

They are most visible at Luneta Park where most domestic workers relax during their day off (Sunday) to meet friends and town mates. SUMAPI members distribute flyers and facilitate flip chart orientations for anyone interested, systematically combing through hundreds of people in the area, at the risk of being branded as fronts for illegal recruitment agencies themselves.

Establishing a conspicuous presence in a public park, where people from all walks of life go, is nothing less than difficult. SUMAPI started in 1995 as a ragtag band of rescued abused domestic workers who were convinced that others could be prevented from falling into a similar fate if they were aware of their rights and entitlements under the law.

A diminutive and shy but uncompromising figure, Chedita Marayag was elected as the first President of the association. Her experience gave her courage and helped her relate effectively with her fellow domestic workers.

"I can easily identify a fellow domestic worker," she beams. At the parks, Chedita would approach a young girl with a casual but deliberate greeting, *"Bisaya ka, 'day?"* ("Are you Visayan?"). In a few minutes, she would blend with a group of park goers, already talking with them about their experiences as housemaids. Her non-threatening, honest personality always disarms a fellow victim into a mood of personal sharing, which ordinary social workers find difficult to achieve given the same opportunity.

The crucial first three minutes of gaining the trust of domestic workers is a moment where former-victims-turned-volunteers like Chedita can be the most effective. Only afterwards would the professional staff of the Visayan Forum intervene. Practical orientation on program services and the legal rights of workers have been designed by social workers and trainers to optimally suit the short attention span and availability of the domestic workers.

The program further gains the trust of most domestic workers through participative and recreational venues, such as volleyball games and fellowship meetings, or simply conveying a warm good-bye as each goes back to her employer for another week of confined work.

While the park outreach with SUMAPI has proven effective in establishing contacts, the real hard work begins at the office each Monday morning. Shoulder to shoulder with the Visayan Forum staff, volunteer CDWs follow up their newfound friends by phone, by mail, and often by personal visits to their workplaces.

Like other children's organizations and other workers' unions, domestic workers' associations face problems such as lack of resources, limited capacity of leaders, unclear direction, minimum participation of members, external threats, among others. Some factors affecting the growth of domestic workers' groups are:

SUMAPI started in 1995 as a ragtag band of rescued abused domestic workers who were convinced that others could be prevented from falling into a similar fate if they were aware of their rights and entitlements under the law.

- ☐ Child domestic workers are available only once a week or twice a month, for 2-3 hours only
- ☐ Fast turnover from one employer to another
- ☐ Scatteredness of workplaces
- ☐ Limited access to outside communication
- ☐ Shyness, or being uneasy in a group
- ☐ Encroachment of park space by other interest groups
- ☐ Mushrooming of entertainment centers and malls which serve as alternatives during days off
- ☐ Employers' refusal to let them join a group

Sustainability Principle 4

Make the invisible visible.

Invisibility is real. As they are historically neglected by society, child domestic workers themselves are not aware of their rights and entitlements, and their productive contributions to society, which make them important.

As supportive institutions, we must help these workers come out and unite to be truly recognized and heard by society. We must help them plant their own seeds of freedom.

Providing broader venues towards genuine participation must have at least the following three-pronged objectives:

1. To expand their social support system towards building resiliency in the face of personal crisis;

2. To advocate for the recognition of their sector, and successfully lobby for the passage of relevant laws such as the Magna Carta; and

3. To develop an intricate network of catchment mechanisms against abuses, illegal recruitment, and the like.

Child domestic workers can be organized in parks, schools, churches, and villages — their natural meeting grounds. We must be creative and interesting in order to catch their attention, and slowly build them into core groups. It is important to encourage the growth of pocket-sized, manageable core groups that address localized needs of individual members.

Ultimately, these groups should be linked together as a massive network on a national scale.

It is effective to first encourage the growth of pocket-sized, manageable core groups to immediately address the localized needs of members. The presence of SUMAPI in alternative schools, for example, has helped create an atmosphere of trust, cooperation, and sharing among domestic workers who normally carry their burdens alone. Organizing SUMAPI in schools and parks prevents CDWs from sliding into working for abusive employers or into other forms of child labor.

There are other places SUMAPI still has not reached. We can apply, for example, the same approach in villages or subdivisions where employers may even approve activities in coordination with local SUMAPI leaders. Constantly monitoring members in the group is also a proactive way of detecting potential abuses.

On a final note, the marginalization of this group of workers, their exclusion from the processes of social change, and their separation as individual victims, all perpetuate their invisibility despite their profusion as an army of unheralded workers. Helping them come out and weaving their threads together will one day make them, at long last, heard.

developing
inner strength

resiliency building

Discovering one's inner strength and recognizing one's own weaknesses as influenced by experiences in the family, community, work and school; unleashing hidden talents and creative energies; tapping family and support networks; honing problem-solving and social skills; constantly reinventing dreams and aspirations; and actualizing daily resolutions as single steps to achieve a big leap — these are hallmarks of resiliency.

These define what and how a person makes informed choices in life. Characteristic of the pliant bamboo, resiliency is indeed a very Filipino trait. This is a core life principle that the *Kasambahay* strategies — especially training, counseling, and SUMAPI organizing — always attempt to inculcate in every child domestic worker.

Developing resiliency factors, both from within and from without, may be the only weapon for the survival of every child domestic worker, especially when external factors, such as employers' attitudes, family expectations, and the economic crunch, are difficult to modify.

The loneliness and outright isolation of these migrant children are eased, if not healed, by regular contact with each other, through telephone calls, visits, letters, and group activities. Through peer and group counseling, they help each other make informed choices. Organizing them into teams and chapters develops and refines their organizational skills in the crucible of practice. It also creates opportunities to make many, many friends. Nor are all activities organizational: they also get together to go to Sunday mass service, watch a movie, or just to talk, to laugh, to play.

The Visayan Forum has codified the concept of resiliency in simple and progressively interrelated themes to make trainings more effective and easy to replicate. Trainers employ creative and participative methods by way of integrated arts to release participants' expressive talents and to touch base with one's cultural roots. Sometimes, trainings are staggered, shortened, deepened, added on, and developed, depending on the time availability and comprehension of participants. The themes of the Basic Processing Seminar for all child domestic workers who avail of trainings for the first time are:

I AM...

A child, and a child domestic worker (includes discussing and processing their experiences and perceptions about work, school, family, and community life. All life stories are interconnected with others

Similar and different from others (involves guiding them through a creative journey of self-discovery about their inner strengths and weaknesses as reflected in their experiences)

I HAVE...

An individual sense of what is right and wrong, and can therefore make informed choices in the face of realities around me

A constellation of supportive (and destructive) people and institutions around me. They may include employers, parents, social workers, friends and relatives, police, teachers, priests, GOs, and NGOs.

Children's rights and entitlements as accorded by law and practice

Roles, responsibilities and benefits from joining SUMAPI core groups

Developing resiliency factors, both from within and from without, may be the only weapon for the survival of every child domestic worker, especially when external factors, such as employers' attitudes, family expectations, and the economic crunch, are difficult to modify.

I CAN / I WILL...

Freely create and pursue my own dreams and ambitions (life plan)

Be an active member of SUMAPI, and immediately do these things...

Formulate daily resolutions as single steps towards a giant leap (such as better habits in school, relation with employers, self-confidence and expressions)

The above themes are also incorporated in *Kasambahay* school retreats that are coordinated with school authorities. The results and evaluation of each retreat are fed back to the concerned teacher, principal, or counselor to guide them in supporting the child domestic worker at school.

Developing resiliency is, of course, a life-long struggle. Realizing truths about one's self and gaining a sense of community reflection towards inter-subjectivity is boosted by attending group trainings. (Inter-subjectivity here means seeing a phenomenon such as personal attitudes, perceptions and habits not only from one's own standpoint but also from that of others). Training and group reflection are therefore very important activities in enhancing individual resiliency.

The other equally important trainings designed and implemented by the *Kasambahay* Program are outlined below. Despite the varying emphasis of their objectives, it should be noted that they all revolve around the basic theme of resiliency.

Rights education field workshops are conducted at parks and school waiting areas with the use of flipcharts and other visual materials. Involving field games, situational discussions, and songs, these workshops increase participants' awareness of the *Kasambahay* Program; encourage sharing of their experiential perceptions on work, school, family and migration; and discuss actual life situations when they needed to make informed choices about their lives, especially in protecting their rights and entitlements.

Para-legal and Social Security System orientation takes up core provisions of the *Batas Kasambahay*, hoping to spark discussion of their terms of conditions at work. Facilitators explain, in layman's terms, effective methods and channels in seeking solutions on work-related problems so that child domestic workers can make informed decisions for themselves and for others. The training equips participants with the skills to document and prepare legal affidavits so that they can proactively participate in seeking legal redress.

Leadership training seminars are advanced seminars designed for participants to: self-discover leadership qualities; acquire learning in organizational planning and assessment, including increased know-how in conflict management; and aid them in long-term planning for their SUMAPI chapters and core groups.

Speakers' pool training is another yearly seminar. Geared for selected SUMAPI leaders, it: clarifies basic messages in advocacy; simulates campaign scenarios; and increases their knowledge about child labor and children's rights in general.

The Visayan Forum trainings for *kasambahays* are not limited to the above examples. We have also made modules that are flexible and adaptable to their situations. In conducting these modules, we learned so many things from them and from the experience itself. Following are some of the lessons we learned while implementing these trainings.

First, we needed more opportunities to encourage the development of each individual child domestic worker's resiliency. Lack of access to the child domestic workers after a training is a real limitation we have to face. But if we look deeper into the lives and experiences of these children, we find a treasure trove of experiences which can teach them about life choices. In this regard, we consider them special because of the trials they undergo.

Second, much of the processing really depends on the emotional intelligence and creativity of the facilitator. Tuning in to their sensitivities is as important as encouraging effective communication. Facilitators should develop a high level of maturity and multiple skills, which continue to evolve only if they regularly conduct trainings among child domestic workers.

Finally, the growth of individual resiliency will always be affected by outside factors no matter how much we emphasize personal choices. The proper context of resiliency for child domestic workers is therefore a critical analysis of the existing employer-employee relationship around which her life as a child and as a worker revolves. This is her present and continuing world that influences her personal growth everyday.

> if we look deeper into the lives and experiences of these children, we find a treasure trove of experiences which can teach them about life choices. In this regard, we consider them special because of the trials they undergo.

Sustainability Principle 5

Improve employer-employee relationship is central to any analysis and intervention for any child domestic worker.

As of the moment this is the only possible intervention that can directly impact the life of the child domestic worker. Many of the dilemmas attached to domestic work spring from the relationship between employers and their CDWs. The range of existing interactions and the roles played by both parties revolves around key themes:

First, abusive tendencies of employers and even slave-like practices are still common today.

Second, many employers mistakenly burden CDWs with adult expectations and often turn a blind eye to these children's rights to education, leisure and socialization.

Third, there is still weak social control affecting this relationship because it is curtained by the privacy of the employers' home.

In order to foresee sustainable ends in outside efforts to aid distressed parties (which may also include employers themselves), the fabric of the employer-employee relationship must ultimately be refined.

The *Batas Kasambahay* captures the necessary improvements by proposing formal conduct leading to professional partnership in the home.

While developing resiliency among child domestic workers is important, employers should also do the same. We believe that there is still a great deal of leeway for child domestic workers and their employers to nurture the relationship with more personal and familistic attitudes.

tools
for social change

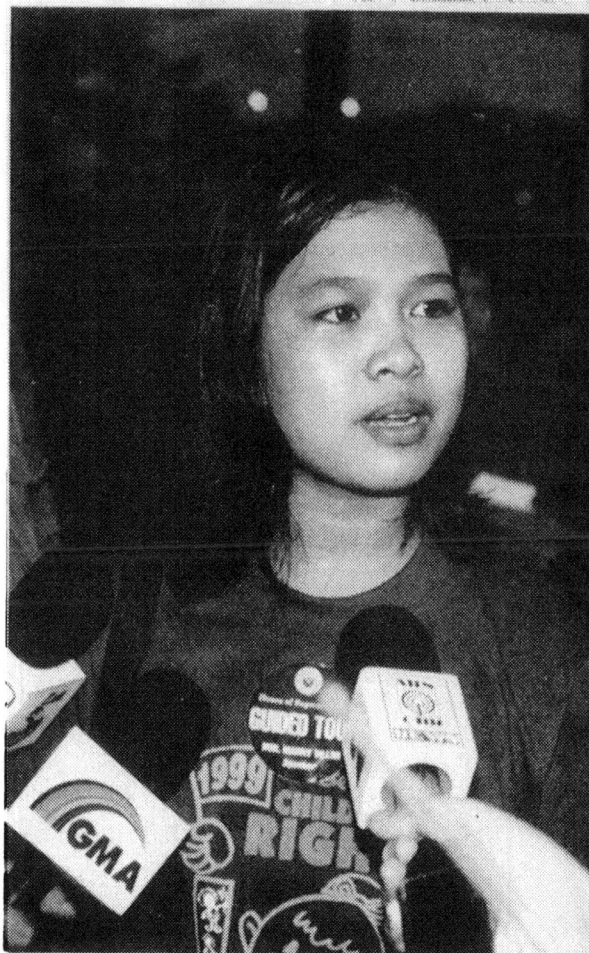

advocacy, lobby work and networking

The Visayan Forum has consistently proposed the use of the term *kasambahay* or household partner to redefine the long-standing and degrading terms indicative of society's low regard for domestic workers. Through a name- recall tactic, we brought the public's consciousness of the social role of domestic workers to the surface, and enabled a closer examination of their situation.

Looking back on our past experience, our advocacy work may have been effective in changing people's perceptions and inspiring urgency and sentiments on the issue of child domestic workers. But we have to raise our advocacy to a higher level of commitment, and translate it into reforms that lead to concrete action at all levels of society.

Advocacy should target a specific audience as advocates who carry the messages that persuade others to see things differently. For us, advocacy means not only raising awareness, but also influencing decision makers — especially legislators — to come up with regulations that can improve the work and life situation of domestic workers in general.

Influencing the perceptions and actions of persons and groups that significantly affect the everyday lives of child domestic workers requires solid analysis and rich insights from real life situations. We need to present the real faces of child domestic workers themselves, employers, and government, among others, so that the process of social dialogue genuinely occurs at many levels of social interaction.

Given the limited resources for advocacy, the Visayan Forum understands very well that it can only target a limited but critically important audience. This includes employers, child domestic workers, legislators, and labor inspectors. In this section, we only discuss ideas central to employers and child domestic workers.

Core message for employers

Whether on television, over the radio or during personal counseling, the Visayan Forum advocates are trained to impart the following Core Message to Employers. It is not complete for every situation but is relatively tight enough to sling our efforts with the proper aim.

"Not all employers are bad. There are also good and well-meaning employers of household helpers who may even be victims of "bad" domestic workers who indiscriminately leave work. By improving the employer-employee relationship, many of the problems that emanate from unmet expectations can be avoided and reduced.

"Our own domestic workers free many of us to work in better paying jobs, so it is high time we give back what they deserve through better working arrangements and humane treatment. We as a nation have demanded better treatment of our overseas contract workers. We should treat our own in at least the same manner.

"As guardians, you should recognize that you have more influence and decision-making power over your domestic worker — more than any other person in her life. Use this influence wisely and lovingly.

"By giving better pay and benefits, humane treatment, more leveled expectations and even continuing education,

Quick Tips in Relating with the Media

- ☐ Relating with the media needs a lot of knowledge, skills and charisma.
- ☐ It is important to understand the press: to know what they want, and how and when to feed it to them.
- ☐ Media seeks to inform, entertain, shape opinion, and capture audience share.
- ☐ In relating to media people, consider that they face deadlines.
- ☐ They are exposed to more information than they seek, and they always remember negative experiences.
- ☐ It is also important to thank them and develop friendly relations with them.

we can help develop our local heroes, who cook our food, guard our houses, host our visitors, and most importantly, act as second parents and friends of our own children.

"Nurture these caregivers the way you want them to deal with your children, especially when you are not around. In fact, many of the habits your children develop may have been copied from their baby-sitters.

"Give your helpers humanity, and in return they will give you loyalty and productivity."

Effective Approaches in Relating with Employers

While it is always important to emphasize to employers the legal provisions pertaining to minimum standards, being too legalistic in our approach to them invites a certain natural resistance. Many employers generally view employing a domestic worker as a personal affair confined to the home.

The Visayan Forum believes in applying the classic principles of punishment to set an example for other abusive employers. However, it equally channels its advocacy towards creatively striking other vital chords in the employers' psyche, using positive reinforcement. This is very effective, most especially when we deal with them face to face. We recognize the following factors, so we fine-tune our messages accordingly.

Familistic values are still the dominant theme in a largely traditional society such as the Philippines. Therefore, we always challenge employers to treat child domestic workers as an integral part of the family, partners in our home, and not merely replaceable servants.

Most Filipinos are religious. In this light, the influence of religious organizations is indispensable. Priests and pastors, who are among our most powerful advocates, shape their sermons to parishioners on the reciprocity theme, "Do unto others as you would like others to do unto you."

In terms of child abuse, we need not go outside our home to find abused children. We may find them within our own backyards. We might as well become good examples, by being good employers to CDWs. While there are many advocacy strategies that capitalize on shame, we can more importantly plant reinforcements that challenge employers to live by their good name and social standing in the community in order to effect changes in their relationship with child domestic workers.

At times it is necessary for us to clearly and directly outline what employers can do immediately. They need specific suggestions on what "humane" is. They need reliable, recognized minimum standards. Some employers, even when, for example, they are paying more than average wages and have registered their domestic worker with the SSS, doubt that they are doing enough. Employers in general, depending on their means, tend to be very subjective about "minimum standards" and what "humane" is.

For CDWs: core message and feedback analysis

SUMAPI is very small compared to the population of domestic workers in the country. The Visayan Forum cannot involve all CDWs in its resiliency training, nor can it reach everybody so they can access direct services. The greater challenge is to touch the lives of the child domestic workers not yet reached, even without ever meeting them.

This is possible using various media. Radio has the widest reach among child domestic workers, especially in urban centers. They always tune in to their favorite FM station while working. While at rest or cooking, they watch television. Melodramas are popular, but we are also amazed by their receptivity to the news. They give feedback, and some of the hindrances we learned from their feedback are as follows:

First, they fear at becoming the source of damage in the employer-employee relationship once they assert their rights. CDWs generally avoid direct confrontation. During days off, for example, they try not to offend their employers by taking time off only in the afternoon. Facing serious offences, child domestic workers tend not to fight back for fear of immediate retaliation or for lack

of an immediate support network. A feeling of personal
indebtedness (utang na loob) also hinders many of them
from asserting their rights.

Second, those working in the city for the first time tell
us that they see themselves as undergoing a period of
adjustment. Having a strict or abusive employer is part of
the learning process. Resistance is futile. Learning to adopt
also implies breaking the language divide and dancing with
the ways and habits of employers.

Recognizing that many child domestic workers are
stuck with this type of coping mechanism, our core
messages used in advocacy are designed to correct this
mindset. So our storyline goes:

"Working at a young age is a reality. Many CDWs
work in somebody else's home, away from home, to help
their parents, to send brothers and sisters to school, for a
chance to study, or simply, to be one mouth less to feed in
the family.

"While others may be forced by poverty, sheer hope
for a secure source of cash, or simply to see the city, we
understand this as the reality: you, at a tender age, are now
working, when in fact you should be in school, when you
should be with your family. But we are not against
children working. We recognize the complexity of
conditions that led you to make your choice to work.

"But when you are in danger while working; when
somebody denies you your right to a decent childhood,
outside contact, proper schooling, or simply a day out for
fun; when you are subjected to abuses that amount to
physical, mental, even sexual torture, or death — we
believe this is not part of the reality called work.

"You are a partner of every Filipino family, helping 24
hours a day, seven days a week. But when you get sick,
who takes care of you? When in dire need of cash or
during emergencies, to whom will you run? Where will
you flee for safety when abused?

"If you want to know more about your rights, and if
you plan to have more chances to develop lifelong skills
and to explore what you can be, we are here to help. Be

part of our work! Because you are true partners, not slaves, at home."

Sustainability Principle 6

Reaffirm the right to decent work and recognize that CDWs are in fact productive members of society.

Young people desire to be recognized as productive members of society. Working is a common way to gain identity and social acceptance.

Domestic work is comparably a light occupation and easy to go into. One does not even have to present a diploma to be hired.

But there are many conditions that make it severely damaging to a child's physical, mental and social development. Many of the hazardous conditions defined in ILO Convention 182 can be found in the everyday situation of child domestic workers.

In this light, the *Batas Kasambahay* sets minimum provisions for the employment of domestic workers of minority age, apart from the broader articles that cover domestic work in general, thus reflecting a proactive approach to the issue. Such provisions include:

- ☐ Setting the allowable age of employment from 15-17 years old

- ☐ Not considering the children of domestic workers as domestic workers themselves

- ☐ Limiting normal hours of work to 10 hours

- ☐ Prohibiting night work

- ☐ Illegalizing hazardous work, activities and working conditions

- ☐ Having their rights to the wages they earn

- ☐ Making emergency services more accessible to them

- ☐ Beefing up resources for repatriation

- ☐ Mandating institutions that can exercise custody over child domestic workers

It remains consistent with the minimum employment age provisions in the country, which prohibit the hiring of children below 15 years old.

lobbying for
policies and
legislative
framework

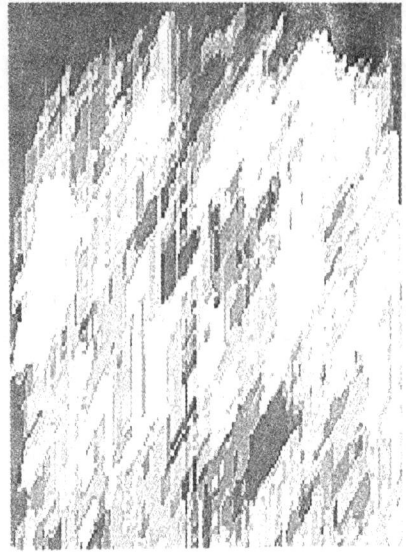

batas kasambahay

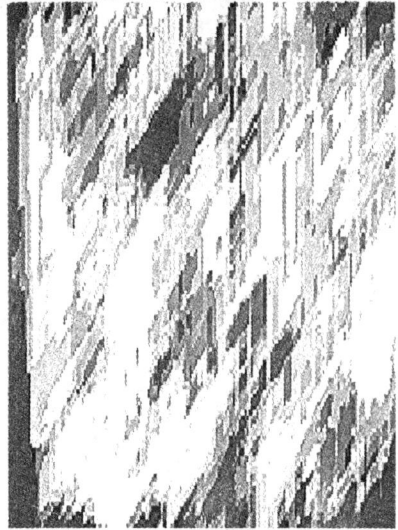

The *Batas Kasambahay* (Domestic Workers' Bill) is by far the most concrete contribution to the legislative needs of domestic workers. It was an initial response to the documentary film *Nakatagong Kasambahay* (Hidden Domestic Workers), aired over primetime television. In its germinal form, it was evidently reactive to perceived gaps of existing and related laws. Some also observed that the bill tended to assume that by expanding the roles and functions of institutions, mainly government, this social dysfunction will be resolved.

When the Visayan Forum started to coordinate with the office of Congressman Jack Enrile who sponsored the bill, we expressed our keenness to share our grassroots experiences in dealing with the everyday problems of child domestic workers, employers, parents, and most especially the institutions that implement programs for CDWs. It is our belief that policies must be based on the experiences of the very people they affect.

A second draft of the bills was developed through the efforts of the solon, the Visayan Forum, ILO-IPEC, Ateneo Human Rights Center, and the Bureau of Women and Young Workers (BWYW) of the DOLE.

Increased minimum wage, 13th month pay, regular days off, wider social security protection, and better working conditions — these benefits normally accorded to formal workers are enshrined in the Magna Carta, which proposes to recognize the contributions of local domestic helpers to national development.

These are the first steps in breaking the historical neglect and exclusion of these workers.

Taking on the interest of domestic workers does not necessarily mean sacrificing the interests of employers. Instead, the Magna Carta also protects employers, by ensuring better relations with domestic workers based on humane treatment and reasonable expectations.

It also protects thousands of minors who are victims of verbal, physical and sexual abuse and illegal recruitment. It encourages employers to continue supporting their child domestic workers' development through training and continued education.

Judging from the various consultations done in many parts of the country, the Visayan Forum believes that the Magna Carta enjoys wide acceptance, even though it has yet to be passed into law. In fact, many employers who have heard of it are beginning to practice very important provisions of the bill. However, it must first be enacted into law before penalties can be imposed on errant employers.

It is not a perfect magna carta. It is not by far a complete blueprint that can address the complexity of the phenomenon. But it is a leap from the long-standing historical neglect and silence on the sector. It is law that can catapult future laws.

Enrile says in his explanatory note: "Let it not be construed, however, that the *Batas Kasambahay* will fully correct the societal imbalance prevalent in this sector, for the circumstances are so complex and the interrelationships so intricate. But we have to start somewhere. Let (it) be the springboard by which other laws that seek to protect the interests of our fellow Filipinos are enacted."

Some consulted sectors have second thoughts about its applicability, judging from the existing mandates of government agencies to implement the services it requires. The issues include non-traditional methods of outreach for SSS registration, availability of funds for repatriation, and existing centers for abused child domestic workers. The expanded role of NGOs and other civil society groups as legal third parties is welcome.

Ultimately, domestic work must be valued as a dignified profession, one which even employers will think twice about corrupting.

Sustainability Principle 7

Constantly improve domestic workers' productivity requires more attention than it received in the past.

Many domestic workers view their work as transitory; very few stay long enough for a single employer. Many employers, in turn, have become suspicious of young workers presenting themselves because experience tells them they are only using the opportunity as a stepping stone for other remunerative jobs in the city. These trends are a far cry from past practice, when maids served their masters as their lifetime vocation.

These trends reflect the belief that domestic work is a peripheral occupation, demand for which increases as employers feel it is cheaper for them to hire a domestic worker, and demand for which may decrease as legislation calls for higher pay and more benefits.

Conversely, the supply of children willing to work in domestic service may increase as young people increasingly drop out of school and more families become economically disenfranchised. The supply may decrease as they become more ready to compete for other higher-paying jobs in the city.

In this light, increasing the salaries and social security coverage of domestic workers is only a first step to ensuring peaceful employer-employee relations. Employers naturally expect more hours of work and heavier loads from their domestic workers once they provide such improvements. This is a common mistake that often leads domestic workers to seek other jobs or employers.

Sustaining these improvements requires that the productivity of domestic workers be developed, compensatory to the benefits they seek. Other employers naturally equate increased productivity with extra training on the culinary arts, food preparation, baby-sitting, and other skills, which is basically self-serving for employers themselves.

Domestic workers should be free to access opportunities for self-improvement, such as continuation of formal schooling, interpersonal management, or training on vocational skills preparatory to alternative jobs other than in the home.

Many employers who were able to support their domestic workers' graduation from domestic work after many years of loyal service feel understandably proud in being instrumental in the transformation of their "family member" into a more productive member of the workforce.

10 fundamental rights of domestic workers

In the event that *Batas Kasambahay* is enacted, the fundamental rights of maids, gardeners, babysitters and caregivers bring this traditionally informal sector closer towards the benefits and protection accorded by law through the following:

Humane Treatment

Domestic workers shall be treated in a just and humane way. Verbal and physical abuse, imprisonment inside the home, or forcibly making them render services in other homes is absolutely unacceptable.

Basic Needs

According to the capacity of the employers, domestic workers are to be provided with a clean place to stay, enough food, and medical attention in case of sickness due to work.

Security

A contract should be signed indicating that the employment will not last more than two years, as an official document for ending services or any relationship with the employer.

Standard Pay and 13th-Month Pay

In Metro Manila, the monthly salary should not be below PhP1,200; and PhP1,000 in all other first class cities and municipalities; PhP900 for the rest. In addition, 13th month pay is mandatory in the amount of the monthly salary; there should be yearly pay increases. Payment shall be made directly to the domestic worker without any deductions unless agreed upon by the employer and domestic worker through a written agreement. The domestic worker will not shoulder any expense including transportation fares, recruitment or finders' fees, and medical examination fees.

Prescribed Hours of Work

No domestic worker will work more than 10 hours a day, exclusive of one-hour breaks for meals. The employer will duly compensate any work rendered by the domestic worker beyond the ten hours accordingly. The domestic worker shall be allowed at least 8 continuous hours of rest per day.

Regular Working Days

No domestic worker shall render work for more than 6 days per week, or rest for less than 4 days per month. While the specific day of the week set aside as the domestic worker's rest day may be stipulated in the employment contract, the same may be exchanged for another day of the week upon the mutual agreement of the domestic worker and the employer as the exigencies of the household may dictate. Domestic workers are also entitled to a 14-day vacation leave with pay annually, and a maternity leave.

Protecting Minors

Although the law allows youths 15 to 17 years old to work as domestic workers, it is illegal to engage them in working environments hazardous to their well being, health and morality. It is unlawful to hire anyone below fifteen years of age.

SSS & Philhealth Membership

Domestic workers should be covered by the Social Security (SSS) and Philippine Health Insurance Corporation (PhilHealth) and enjoy the benefits provided by these agencies. To facilitate this, the SSS launches outreach programs for domestic workers.

Self Development

It is the right of every domestic worker to strive for self-development and education as allowed by her work schedule. This right will not be a precedent for any deductions from the domestic worker's salary. There will be no domestic worker below legal age denied of formal or vocational education.

Participation

The privacy of domestic workers shall be respected at all times, especially during their rest periods and concerning personal communication outside of the employer's house. No domestic worker will be hampered from seeking the assistance of legal representatives like the Department of Labor and Employment (DOLE), barangay council or registered non-government organizations. As one way to give them due recognition for their contribution to society, the *"Araw ng mga Kasambahay"* (Domestic Workers Day) will be observed as a non-working holiday with pay.

attacking the roots of the cdw issue

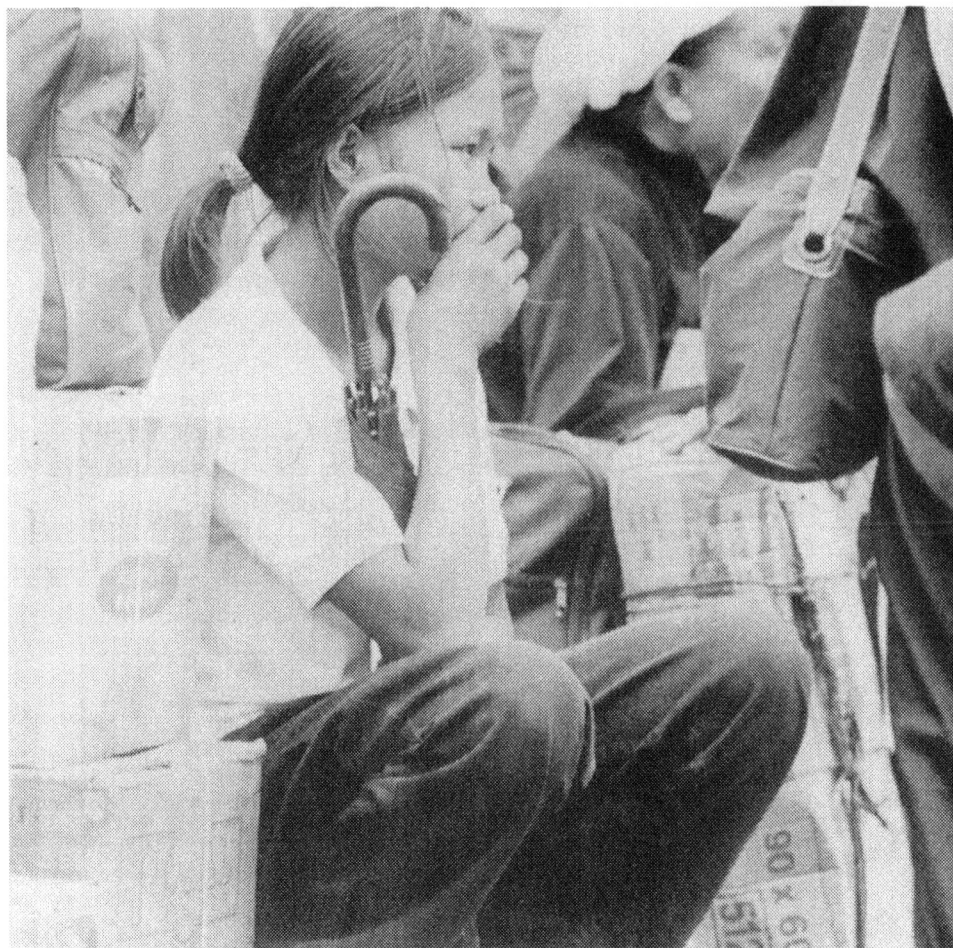

prevention work

During a final feedback session for a thematic evaluation of the *Kasambahay* Program, a consultant asked the Visayan Forum team, "If you were to start all over again, knowing what you know now about child domestic workers, how would you do your work?"

The answer was unanimous. We all felt that the wisest thing to do was more preventive work. We wanted to decrease the reasons why thousands of children enter the system. Our experiences with various strategies tell us that it is very difficult to help children when much damage has been done.

Prevention is addressing the root causes before any child goes into the system. But we are not about to judge whether the system of child domestic work needs to be totally uprooted. It can be both a boon and a bane, depending on what part you are looking at. This is the paradox of the phenomenon.

A practical perspective is to recognize that even with the many effective ways of addressing these root causes, the phenomenon of child domestic work will not vanish overnight. We should develop more strategies that we can do at multiple levels, such as:

- Working at source or sending communities, from where child domestic workers are recruited;
- Checking child domestic workers' step migration from one city to another, from one employer to another;
- Helping child domestic workers in danger during transit, at embarking and disembarking points such as ports, bus stations, and border check points;
- Preventing them from entering or being stuck in abusive employment situations; and
- Averting child domestic workers' slide into worse forms of child labor.

Aside from working at source or sending communities, the *Kasambahay* Program does all these strategies. Apart from these, the Visayan Forum also implements successful preventive programs in selected regions and communities.

Implementing the provisions of ILO Convention 138, which the country ratified in 2000, will dramatically help in prevention. Government has been providing the necessary enabling environment, though there are still many things that must be done:

☐ Prevent the engagement of children in the worst conditions of domestic work

☐ Provide direct assistance for the removal, rehabilitation and integration of child domestic workers already in hazardous conditions

☐ Ensure access to free basic education and vocational training for all

☐ Enact policies to enable an environment that protects both the interests of employers and domestic workers

Sustainability Principle 8

Work for a blanket ban on child domestic work for those below 15 years.

Requiring children to perform adult tasks, especially child-rearing, separating them from their natural family at an age when they cannot yet make truly informed choices about their lives, making them easy targets of illegal recruiters, and allowing them to fall into the hands of unknown employers whose domestic practices may border on child abuse — these are reasons enough to discourage and penalize the recruitment of children below 15 years of age into domestic work.

One may argue that relatives may have the noblest aims in "adopting" less privileged kin. Perhaps they wish to send the child to school, an opportunity her own parents may not be able to afford. Maybe a couple takes pity on a child running away from abusive parents and take her in as their own.

But these are not enough reasons to justify the employment of the very young. Guardians commonly require the "adopted" child to perform chores, with no pay at all. Most "adopted" child domestic workers are still treated as workers. Without having to abide by the formalities of government-accredited adoption schemes, many guardians distort the very principles of this arrangement.

**Kasambahay Program
Chronology of Events**

1995
May	Program commencement with ILO-IPEC support
June	Start of field outreach activities at Luneta Park
December	First General Assembly of SUMAPI

1996
April	Conduct of Research on CDWs in Batangas, Cebu and Davao
June	Filing of a Senate Bill for Domestic Workers by Senator Francisco Tatad
August	First National Consultation on CDWs in the Philippines

1997
February	Program expansion in Bacolod (Visayas)
May	Program expansion in Davao (Mindanao)
November	First Regional Consultation on CDWs in Asia

1998
January	Global March Against Child Labor kick-off in Manila
January	Program expansion in Batangas (Luzon)
June	Participation in the Global March culmination in time for the deliberation of ILO Convention 182 at the ILC
August	Formation of the Child Laborers and Advocates for Social Participation (CLASP)

1999
April	Filming of Out of Sight, Out of Mind video documentary
June	Lobbying for the Adoption of ILO Convention 182
August	Licensing of VF by the Department of Social Welfare and Development
September	Clarified issues prior to the release of DOLE Department Order No. 4 on Hazardous Work to Children
December	Filing in Congress of the Magna Carta for Domestic Workers

2000

January	Conduct of Research: Situational Analysis on Trafficking at the Manila Port
April	Launching of the first-ever *Araw ng mga Kasambahay* (Domestic Workers Day)
July	Inauguration of Port Halfway House (for trafficked children)
August	Conduct of Thematic Evaluation on CDWs in the Philippines by ILO-IPEC
December	Ratification of ILO Convention 182 in the Philippines

2001

January	Start of Monthly Mass SSS Registration for Domestic Workers
April	*Araw ng mga Kasambahay* in Davao
May	*Araw ng mga Kasambahay* in Bacolod
June	Refiling of *Batas Kasambahay* in the 12th Congress
July	Renewal of MOA with PPA, extending the term for the halfway house operation for 5 years and expanding to other major ports in the Philippines
July	Start of tri-weekly TV advocacy: Household Help portion at *Unang Hirit*

"Ultimately, justice for child domestic workers
rests upon changes in the very fabric of society,
specifically in its valuation of children, of women,
and of domestic work."

part 4

clarion call

a glimpse of the ocean

the ocean

issues and challenges

It has not been easy for us at the Visayan Forum to trace, discover, and appreciate the lessons from our past successes as well as our past failures. On the other hand, we are aware of the issues and challenges that working with child domestic workers teaches us. This book's preface alluded to our achievements as a small ripple in these children's ocean of misery. We now offer you a glimpse of that ocean.

Justice

As we have previously discussed, existing laws are scattered, inadequate and antiquated. We must make changes that go beyond codifying these laws. *Batas Kasambahay*, as laudable a breakthrough as it is in codifying, improving and adding to existing provisions relevant to children domestic workers, is but a first step. The Visayan Forum, however, realizes that it has no mandate to set parameters of moral and social codes for legislative formulations. What it does is develop allies among policy makers, in the hopes of influencing their legislative agenda to include the interests of child domestic workers.

Nor can we define laws and leave it at that. The existing machinery investigating, monitoring, regulating and acting on the presence and conditions of children in the domestic workplace must be enabled to effectively implement the law. Laws not applied, like justice delayed, also result in justice denied. Without the machinery necessary and capable of enforcing laws and regulations, *Batas Kasambahay* may be passed and yet turn out as a mockery of domestic workers' prayers for justice.

Most child domestic workers who ask for help suffer abuse of their rights as children — and as women. Under international law, the state has clear responsibility for human rights abuses committed by non-state actors: people and organizations acting outside the state and its organs. When a state demonstrates complicity, acquiescence, failure to exercise due diligence and to provide equal protection in preventing and punishing such abuses by private individuals, the state is allowing violence against women and children to continue. This is a failure of state protection. State inaction can be seen in inadequate preventive measures; police indifference to abuses; failure to define abuses as criminal offences; gender bias in the court system; and legal procedures which hamper fair criminal prosecution.

Ultimately, justice for child domestic workers rests upon changes in the very fabric of society, specifically in its valuation of children, of women, and of domestic work. Unless we make *Batas Kasambahay* a way of life, a national habit, involving not only legally mandated bodies but all households whether or not they either employ or have a member who is employed as a child domestic worker, all that these children have struggled for will come to naught.

Case Story: Cita

Cita, then 16 years old, barely lived to tell her story. According to hospital records, she suffered from severe internal bleeding caused by acid burns. Portions of her back and legs were also burned, indicating her struggles during the incident. Acid also burned her entire digestive system from the esophagus down to the stomach. She literally could not speak about her ordeal, and could not swallow food. After several months of hospital therapy and successive operations, she began to confide in her doctors. She stated that she was tricked by her employer into drinking an acid normally used to unclog kitchen drains. She summoned the last of her strength to file a case of attempted homicide against her employer. Cita died the day after she signed her complaint.

Trafficking

When discussing the issue of trafficking, most NGOs, development workers, researchers and even government authorities look at trafficking in the context of child prostitution. This perception must be expanded, since in reality, trafficked children are usually promised jobs as domestic workers at their place of destination. In fact, trafficked children end up not only in prostitution, but also as workers in domestic service, factories and other service sectors that are mostly considered as hazardous work. It is therefore important to look into the practice of trafficking as a whole.

Generally, trafficking is defined as the recruitment and, potentially, the transportation of persons within or across borders by use of deception, force or coercion. We at the Visayan Forum adopt the definition of the UN Protocol on Trafficking: it is "the recruitment, transportation, transfer, harboring or receipt of persons by means of the threat or use of force or other forms of coercion, abduction, fraud, deception, the abuse of power or a position of vulnerability, or the giving or receiving of payments or benefits to achieve the consent of a person having control over another person, for the purpose of exploitation, including prostitution or other forms of sexual exploitation, forced labor, slavery, or practices similar to slavery and servitude."

In the Philippines, typical domestic workers are usually migrants trafficked by deceptive recruiters from poor agricultural or fishing communities in the islands and provinces. Annually, an average of 3-5 million passengers go through the Manila North Harbor. Of these, more than half are estimated to be women and children in search of work and opportunity.

There is a high incidence of deceptive recruitment and trafficking for work, including cross-border movement. A huge number are recruited through the combination of deception, false promises and cash incentives. They continue to increase in number. The human Diaspora pumps day and night, powered by a well-organized network of contacts oiled by good connections between unscrupulous agencies and government authorities. Most of the contracts and birth certificates are often fabricated to attest to the lawfulness of their recruitment. These migrant workers, mostly women and children, experience different problems and different forms of abuse.

Those who are victims of illegal recruiters are forbidden from contacting people outside the group. They frequently have only sketchy information on who will meet them: just a name, or a picture, or an old phone number. Some are stranded for hours, some for days, and some permanently. Fetchers do not show on time, or are misinformed about arrival schedules; many migrants simply have no contacts and linger at the ports; some cannot afford return passage; fixers and robbers steal their money. Few opt to return, saying that it is "shameful to go back hungry and penniless."

Scheming taxi drivers, fellow passengers, and even illegal recruiters posing as social workers or good Samaritans prey on them. Port authorities cannot intervene unless a passenger complains. As they say, "We are in the business of moving people, not hampering their exercise of their constitutional right to freedom of movement." Thus, they can intercept, at the ports of origin, under-aged passengers suspected of being illegally transported. But they cannot apprehend perpetrators. They can shelter these passengers only for 24 hours, or until somebody legally claims them. Except for dining and waiting areas, ports lack facilities for stranded or intercepted passengers.

Once these children leave the port area or bus station, they may simply vanish, absorbed into invisible or illegal work. It becomes nearly impossible to reach them and monitor their situation. Services should be available and intervention should be done in these places, before they are moved beyond the reach of services, of intervention, and of all our good intentions.

Case Story: Agnes

Agnes, 12, is the fifth of 8 children. She is skinny and frail and looks 5 years younger than her age. She hails from a remote town in Southern Philippines. She was recruited to work as a domestic worker in Manila by a certain Edna, who handed PhP 1,000 to Agnes' parents. "I have been working as a domestic worker since the age of 7, for my grade school teacher. I'd rather take my chances in Manila rather than be just another mouth to feed here."

Three of Agnes' older siblings are all in Manila, all as domestic workers. They, too, started working at a very young age. Though her mother was hesitant to permit Agnes to go at first, she was convinced by the thought that Agnes would be visited by her older brother and sisters in Manila.

When Agnes finally arrived in Manila, she was locked at the agency office where Edna brought her for 3 days. Fortunate to have the telephone number of her older sister, she called for help. The following day, she was released from possible trafficking for prostitution, upon payment of her transportation expenses, plus the advance payment given to her parents.

Child domestic work and child labor

When we talk about child labor, we should always use as framework the UN Convention on the Rights of the Child, which generally provides a broader perspective on the latter's rights and needs. Child labor is child work that is exploitative, socially unjust and hazardous, where children are deprived of proper education and normal health.

While much attention is given to more obvious forms of child labor — such as mining, street children, and prostitution — CDWs are largely forgotten. Because they are scattered and invisible, child domestic workers are the most difficult type of working children to protect. Working behind closed doors, employed in separate private households, they are barely reached by traditional inspection methods. The exploitative nature of the occupation remains hidden until much damage has been done to the lives of its victims. Their plight continues to be smoke-screened by the universal right to private property, which provides employers dominion over what goes on inside their homes.

Child domestic workers face economic exploitation through onerous terms of employment, as well as abusive conditions of work, and other practices that contravene international standards. Such standards include ILO Conventions No. 29 (Concerning Forced or Compulsory Labor, 1930) and 138 (Concerning the Minimum Age for Admission to Employment, 1973), as well as the UN Supplementary Convention of 1956 (on the Abolition of Slavery, the Slave Trade, and Institutions and Practices Similar to Slavery). At the very least, the conditions that render child domestic work hazardous should be recognized:

☐ The child is separated from her family. She is working away from home.

☐ The child is under the complete control of her employer, who does not necessarily adhere to the child's best interest.

☐ The child can be subjected to extreme forms of verbal, physical and sexual abuse.

- ☐ The child is subjected to long hours of work, and is generally on call all day.
- ☐ The child is underpaid or not paid at all.
- ☐ The child is provided inadequate food and accommodation.
- ☐ The child can be denied access to schooling, and deprived of education and other basic children's rights.

It is neither practical nor realistic to totally ban children from working as a domestic worker, especially those 15-18 years old. Given the magnitude of children involved in this occupation, a total ban can be counterproductive instead, and generally difficult to monitor and implement. The new ILO Convention 182 and Recommendation 190 should be interpreted in the context of the conditions that exploit and abuse child domestic workers. Discussion and advocacy at the international level should be provided by the ILO, especially IPEC, in order to define effective and strong standards. Governments that ratified the convention, such as ours, should also tackle the need to ensure that the exploitative features of child domestic work are addressed in implementing the new convention.

...child labor is inseparable from the economic situation, and from crises accruing from it. It is a response to crisis and has become cultural as well as political.

Furthermore, child labor is inseparable from the economic situation, and from crises accruing from it. It is a response to crisis and has become cultural as well as political. Its persistence throughout history is evidence of the economic crisis the country has been undergoing. The phenomenon of child labor must be explained not only within the confines of the family, household, and community or the institutions and structure of society where it is present. Ultimately, the phenomenon of child labor in any society must be viewed within the wider context of its role in global capitalist accumulation.

Education

Education is considered by many to be one of the most effective interventions against child labor. ILO Convention 182 affirms this, emphasizing the importance of education in eliminating child labor. The World Conference on Education for All in Jomtien (Thailand,

1990) delivered a worldwide consensus on an expanded vision of basic education, along with the commitment to ensure that basic learning needs of all children, youth and adults are met. It recognizes education as both a fundamental right and as essential for overall national development. The EFA Declaration served as the platform that launched a global movement in support of basic education. The World Education Forum in Dakar (Senegal, 2000) provided an opportunity to deliver on the 2015 commitment to universal primary education. Coinciding with that forum was the launching of a global education campaign by international civil society that calls for a global action plan on education.

We believe that the time of the child is now and the time for their development should be now. It is indeed high time to pay more attention to their education. Our educational system fails to absorb, retain, and prepare children for a more productive adulthood. Many things about the present educational system discourage or drive children, especially working children, away. As previously discussed, not all barangays and towns have elementary or secondary schools. Most families cannot provide for the child's school uniform, supplies, and other expenses. Formal schooling is conducted when working children are at work. Methods fail to engage their attention, inspire their creativity, or encourage retention. The development of vocational skills is not given the notice it deserves. Our educational system needs to be fine-tuned to its market's requirements, in terms of access, availability, appropriate schedules, alternative methods, and immediately useful content.

While we continue to lobby for more investment in education, we should also continue to work with the opportunities that we already have. Education is not confined to the four walls of the classroom alone. Children need diverse experiences from the broad spectrum of social ecology for learning. The educational system's potential as a wellspring of positive learning, achievement, preparation for adult life, future work prospects, socialization and development of self-esteem must be activated.

Government, private educators, development workers, child labor activists, community leaders, the teachers and the children themselves must work together towards attaining a realistic, flexible, and relevant education such that we re-establish and redefine its genuine developmental purpose.

Gender

The "invisibility" of child domestic workers also derives from the fact that the majority of them are girls. Doing domestic work in a household other than their own is seen merely as an extension of their duties: the concept of employment is missing. In many value systems, girls' and women's work is still economically disregarded — simply because girls and women do it. Domestic service has been shown as the most common activity of girls as they enter the world of work or leave the world of school. Because many girls are more likely to be working in the home — as their mothers' assistant, as homeworkers, as domestic servants, or even as prostituted children in "foster" homes — not regulating the private sphere actively endangers them.

It is commonly said that "Behind every man's success, there is always a woman." It is not commonly realized, however, that behind every career woman's success, there is another woman or girl — a domestic worker.

These girls free many women employers from housework so that they can become economically productive in the national workforce, a fact openly unrecognized in many societies. It is commonly said that "Behind every man's success, there is always a woman." It is not commonly realized, however, that behind every career woman's success, there is another woman or girl — a domestic worker.

The phenomenon of child domestic work is a women's issue that the women's movement has long ignored in its own struggle for change and reforms. A close examination of the issues involved underscores the importance of this issue for everyone concerned with gender. Gender stereotyping occurs while women are still girls, like these domestic workers who, as the NSO distinguishes, occupy themselves with "housework" while boys "work." With these girls, women's double burden is shared by two females: the woman who works outside the home, and the domestic worker who works inside it. Violence against them, especially verbal and emotional abuse, is so common that it is considered a mere occupational hazard. They are marginalized and subordinated into domestic service, with little hope of escape. Before they can even begin to be called women, their problems are women's problems.

The gender divide between the public and private sphere is strongly related to the phenomenon of child domestic work. As long as domestic work is not a public industry, it will remain as a disreputable, dead-end occupation. As long as domestic work is lowly regarded, the public sphere shall continue to be separate from the private sphere, and these children, male or female, will remain invisible. As long as the value of domestic work is not recognized by society, hard cash and ownership of property will continue to be the merciless measure of a person's worth, and those with very little or none will still be difsmissed as mere "mouths to feed." As long as the privacy of the home bars public scrutiny and responsibility, women and children shall still be prey to abuse and violence in their own homes.

> As long as domestic work is lowly regarded, the public sphere shall continue to be separate from the private sphere, and these children, male or female, will remain invisible.

Unless the women's movement takes up common cause with domestic workers, the division of society into a public and private domain shall persist, and all the gains achieved thus far become empty rhetoric. Domestic work in its entirety is a women's issue.

Statistics

The real number of child domestic workers is difficult to determine due in part to their statistical invisibility. They are statistically invisible because they are children, and because they are engaged in domestic work.

Our government's labor force and employment statistics gather data only regarding citizens at least 15 years old, the legal bottom line for employment. How can government shape policies for the benefit of those below this age limit when it ignores the fact that a significant number of them are already working?

Enterprises employing 10 or less workers are shunted off into the informal sector. Households, as a rule, hire less than 10 workers for domestic service. Thus, they are theoretically part of this sector. However, domestic work is not listed among the industries covered by government definition of this sector. Nor is it included in the occupations considered as part of this sector. Statistics concerning this increasing yet hidden section of the economy do not encompass domestic work, or domestic workers.

Even when government tried to investigate the situation of domestic workers, the data it gathered was limited by several factors characteristic of domestic work: the worker was allegedly or actually a member of the family; the worker was compensated in terms of food, lodging, and schooling, and was thus not considered by the employer as "hired"; employers resisted investigation as a violation of their privacy.

As long as we retain ignorance about this invisible sector, we will also remain ignorant about matters crucial to understanding our economy and our growth as a nation. Specifically, we cannot correctly value the contribution domestic work makes, both directly and indirectly, to our economy. This is especially important since domestic work has been pointed out as a growth multiplier — that is, domestic workers enable a household to contribute much more than it can without them. Parallel with the importance of understanding the role and contribution of the burgeoning informal sector, any understanding and policies made in ignorance of this occupation are bound to result in errors, errors that neither our economy nor our people can bear.

As long as we remain ignorant of the domestic workers' plight, we cannot hope to adequately serve them — whether they number 766,000 (1995) or more likely, nearly 3 million, especially the children who may now be as many as a million. In this way, we lose any moral authority to demand respect and just treatment for our sisters, wives, and mothers working as domestic helpers abroad.

As long as we remain ignorant of domestic work as a phenomenon, we cannot begin to understand why it persists as a marketable occupation despite the technological advances that have almost eradicated it from other countries. Thus we perpetuate a profession that encourages us to be technologically backward, by devaluing and degrading what is necessary and supportive to everything else we do: domestic work.

Development

The phenomenon of child domestic work is also an issue of development because its rise and prevalence is closely related to poverty and underdevelopment. Unbalanced regional growth in the Philippines fuels the engines of younger workers' migration — many of whom enter domestic work as a stepping stone for other job opportunities in cities like Manila. Factors such as globalization and the growth of the middle class, which contribute to the rising demand for children in domestic work, should not be used to justify sidestepping the issue in the national development agenda.

Despite their contribution to societal development, they are not specifically recognized in the formal labor spectrum. They are not included in the government's development agenda. They are not involved in the process of consultation, where they can air their issues and concerns. Above all, their situation is worsened by the societal perception that domestic workers are second-class citizens.

If we consider them as our partners in every Filipino household, it is valuable to include their issues at the development level, like the attention we give to their counterparts abroad, the Overseas Filipino Workers (OFWs) who toil as domestic helpers in foreign households.

The Asian financial crisis hit not only the financial sector, but children of poor families as well. Many poor agricultural and fishing families depend greatly on their children working in urban households for the cash remittances needed to buy necessities and support costs, including the school expenses of their siblings.

We should look at the economic impact of domestic work as a sector in terms of its financial contribution parallel to that of the OFWs. The nature of their contribution is very similar. The only difference is that OFWs contribute in terms of dollars while local domestic workers, including children, contribute in terms of pesos. Taking into account the number of local domestic workers who send money to their families in the provinces, their contribution is probably bigger than the OFWs'. It is ironic that OFWs have regulations and programs for assistance from the government in place, while our local domestic workers have almost nothing to depend on.

Case Story: Rosenda

Rosenda looks younger than her registered age of 15. Abandoned by her mother at birth, she was left in the care of an old woman who persuaded her mother not to abort the child but to give the child to her instead. "I never knew who my real parents were."

She helps her poor adoptive family by doing odd jobs as a domestic helper in her squatter neighborhood. "I fetch water and our neighbors ask me to run errands like buying stuff from the market. Usually I fetch a lot of water. I have to fill up a drum twice heavier than me. Sometimes it's far from the source and they tell me off if I can't manage to do it."

Rosenda is among the many working children who underwent psychosocial processing with Visayan Forum. Being only in second grade does not prevent her from dreaming to become a social worker someday.

... to be treated as persons

recommendations

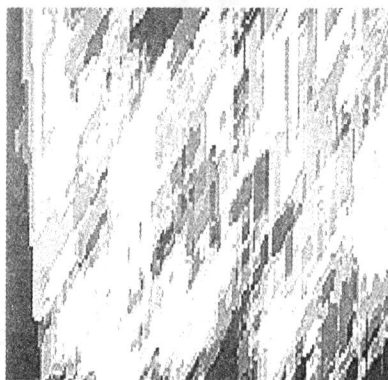

We offer the following groups of recommendations to caregivers, researchers, statisticians and information managers, policy-makers, law enforcers, communities and people's organizations, media, and international organizations and donor agencies. Each of us has a role in the child domestic worker's world. We all have the ability to choose for ourselves how we will continue our involvement: to perpetuate, alleviate, prevent, or eradicate. Over and above all these proposals, let us remind ourselves of the one over-arching desire of these children: to be treated as persons.

For caregivers

We ask all caregivers, from the government, NGOs and civil society, to consider the following actions, which are intended to increase the forms of services that can be offered, expand the number of children that can avail of them, heighten social impact, and encourage sustainability.

☐ Place greater emphasis on all aspects of prevention, particularly direct prevention, and recognize that prevention also involves keeping child domestic workers from being pulled into worse circumstances, such as homelessness and prostitution.

☐ Promote the importance of education and training (formal and non-formal), including education for parents, teachers, employers, workers, field staff, and volunteers. Make education more accessible and relevant to the special needs of child domestic workers.

☐ Create telephone hotlines and other quick response mechanisms.

☐ Coordinate legal protection and enforcement, including the investigation and prosecution of cases of abuse.

☐ Act against deceptive recruitment and trafficking of children into domestic work, especially in entry/exit points, such as bus stations and ports.

- ☐ Set up crisis intervention/welfare/halfway centers that provide holistic programs for needy child domestic workers, such as drop-in facilities/temporary shelter, psychosocial counseling, health monitoring, recreation and services, legal assistance, alternative education/skills trainings, and repatriation services whenever necessary.

- ☐ Develop non-conventional approaches in reaching out to the invisible ones and set up outreach activities in parks, schools, churches and accessible workplaces.

- ☐ Involve child domestic workers at all levels of program implementation and social advocacy.

- ☐ Provide additional interventions for parents and communities to prevent children from migrating for work, such as educational and livelihood programs, medical missions, and other initiatives.

- ☐ Build strategic alliances with various sectors/groups (government agencies, non-government organizations, people's formations, workers, employers, church, academe, media and civil society groups).

- ☐ Advocate for a paradigm shift from vulnerability to competence among caregivers.

For Researchers, Statisticians and Information Managers

We ask all researchers, statisticians and information managers to help make the invisible visible, by considering the following actions.

- ☐ Conduct both quantitative and qualitative studies with working children and their families, under the conditions of ILO 182 / Recommendation 190 using action participatory methods.

- ☐ Develop an accessible and understandable database on the issue.

- ☐ Present models of effective approaches and programs.
- ☐ Determine the magnitude of the sector from NSO surveys. If this is unavailable, work out its inclusion in national surveys.
- ☐ Practice ethics in the conduct of researches, especially sensitivity to children's and women's issues.

For Policymakers

We ask policymakers to consider the following actions, towards a long-term response to the phenomenon of child domestic work.

- ☐ Recognize domestic service as work, and as such, subject to legal provisions and regulation.
- ☐ Integrate domestic work with policies regarding national development, poverty alleviation, social protection and education.
- ☐ Pass *Batas Kasambahay* and enact national policies on domestic work that provide a legal framework for domestic work, including employer-employee relationship, work contract, and social security and health benefits, among others.
- ☐ Encourage voluntary codes of practice concerning the employment of child domestic workers.

For Law Enforcers

We ask law enforcers to increase their current efforts at curbing the worst forms of domestic work, up to and including deceptive recruitment and trafficking, by considering the following actions.

- ☐ Define operational guidelines regarding hazardous and illegal forms of domestic service.
- ☐ Act against deceptive recruitment and trafficking.

- Create hotlines for quick response and as a preventive mechanism.
- Develop coordinated inter-agency monitoring and surveillance strategies, and a non-violent or non-confrontational approach during rescue/pull-out operations.
- Conduct seminars/trainings to sensitize their ranks on the issue.
- Improve the proper and efficient documentation and databasing of cases.

For Communities and People's Organizations

We ask communities and people's organizations to consider the following actions, and in so doing, contribute to preventive efforts on a social scale.

- Mobilize and set up mechanisms to prevent children from going into hazardous circumstances, such as community child-watch systems.
- Influence policies at the level of the barangay and other local government units.
- Develop credibility so as to gain greater access to government services.
- Build partnerships with organizations that promote alternative sustainable livelihoods and extend micro-financing to communities.
- Register child domestic workers at the community level.

For the Media

We ask the media to contribute to social change, by considering the following actions.

- Cover public awareness-raising activities to change the perception of domestic work throughout society.
- Practice responsible journalism and media ethics; observe sensitivity to the issues of domestic work.

For International Organizations / Donor Agencies

We ask international organizations and donor agencies to consider the following actions, which are aimed at strengthening the capability of civil society to change the social fabric that perpetuates child domestic work.

☐ Organize activities for collective action and strengthen solidarity at various levels.

☐ Support organizational initiatives of domestic workers, such as the formation of SUMAPI core groups and chapters.

☐ We call on international agencies, especially the International Labour Organization to have a wider plan for domestic work in general, and pursue domestic work issues in relation to Core Labor Standards and Decent Work, among others; push for the recognition of domestic work as productive work, with a real impact on the national economy; and draw up a logical framework (setting objectives, outputs and indicators) for its work on the phenomenon of child domestic work.

endnotes &
bibliography

endnotes

1   National Statistics Office Labor Force Survey, April 1995 cited by Ma. Alcestis A. Mangahas, *National NGO Consultation on CDWs in the Philippines*, 1996

2   National Statistics Office, Census 2000 Preliminary Results

3   National Statistics Office, Population Projections for 2001, Low Assumption

4   ILO-IPEC, Children in Hazardous Work in the Philippines, 1999

5   National Statistics Office, Labor Force Survey, April 1995

6   National Survey on Working Children, July 1995, Partial and Preliminary Results

7   National Statistical Coordination Board, 1992

8   Jurado and Castro, 1978, cited by Romulo A. Virola in "Measuring the Contribution of the Informal Sector in the Philippines," *NSCB Technical Paper on the Informal Sector* No. 2001-003, March 2001

9   Ibid.

10 1992 Commission on the Filipino Language. *English-Tagalog Dictionary.* Institute of National Language: Pasig, Metro Manila, 1992

11 Rule XIII, Section 1(b), Book 3 of the Philippine Labor Code, as amended

12 *2001 Factsheet,* Department of Education, Culture and Sports

13 Philippine Daily Inquirer, 1998

14 DECS, 2001

15 DOLE-Bureau of Labor Statistics. "Women in Employment: A Profile (1989-1999)," *LabStat,* Vol 4 No. 4, February 2000

16 Ibid.

17 Ibid.

18 Ibid.

19 DOLE-BLES. "The Labor Force Survey In Brief :
    January (1999-2000)", *LabStat,* Vol. 4 No. 6,
    March 2000

20 DOLE-BLES, op. cit., February 2000

21 Ibid.

22 "Clothes for the Rich from the Hands of the Poor",
    Child Workers in Asia, October-December 1993

23 ILO/Department of Labor and Employment.
    Child Labor: Let Us Work Against It, 1996

24 "Children Forced to Work", *ECPAT Bulletin,*
    Vol. 4/1, 1996-97

25 Mante, James S. and Loree Cruz-Mante, *Redefining the
    Strategic Directions and Thrusts of the National Program
    Against Child Labor 2000-2004,* May 2001

26 Ibid.

27 Maggie Black and Jonathan Blagbrough.
    Anti-Slavery International. "First Things First",
    innocenti digest 5. UNICEF, 1999

bibliography

"APEC conference on best practices for eliminating the worst forms of child labor and providing educational opportunities for youth." Bangkok, Thailand: 25-26 October 2000

"Clothes for the Rich from the Hands of the Poor." *Child Workers in Asia,* October-December 1993

"Maid bill gains Congress support," *Sun Star Davao.* 9 April 2000, pp. 3 and 17

"The Wheels of Justice," *National Renewal.* September 1994, p. 20

"Thematic Evaluation: IPEC Interventions on Child Domestic Work, Experience from IPEC-Philippines," IPEC-Philippines, 2000 (draft report)

1992 Commission on the Filipino Language. *English-Tagalog Dictionary.* Institute of National Language: Pasig, Metro Manila, 1992

Abrera-Mangahas, Ma. Alcestis. "Learning by doing: policy and program responses on child domestic work," presented at the Regional Consultation on Child Domestic Workers, 19-23 November 1997

Anti-Slavery International. "Child domestic workers and new International Labour Organization standards on the worst forms of child labour." May 1999

Brillantes, Romulo C. "Consolidated Analysis of the Case Studies on Selected Child Domestic Workers," Bureau of Women and Young Workers Research Division: 2 August 1996

Brillantes, Romulo C. "Review of Legal and Policy Framework on Child Labor / Child Domestics," Bureau of Women and Young Workers, 25 March 1996

Brillantes, Romulo C. "Some Statistics on Child Workers/ Domestic Helpers," Bureau of Women and Young Workers Research Division: 9 May 1996

Brillantes, Romulo C. "Survey on the Working and Living Conditions of Child Domestic Helpers in Metro Manila (Highlights)," Bureau of Women and Young Workers Research Division: 15 May 1996

Bureau of Child and Youth Welfare. *Child Protective Services: A Primer on Child Welfare Services.* Bureau of Child and Youth Welfare: Quezon City, Philippines

Cadacio, Jodeal. "Enrile pushes Magna Carta for maids," *Today.* 8 December 1999, pp. 1 and 12

Canuday, Jowel F. "Government pressed on maids' magna carta," *Philippine Daily Inquirer* 11 April 2000 p. 14

Child Workers in Asia, Vol 16, No. 2 May-August 2000

Department of Education, Culture and Sports *2001 Factsheet*

DOLE Bureau of Working Conditions. *"Mga Karapatan ng Katulong sa Bahay,"* 1997

DOLE Department Order No. 4, Series 1999

DOLE-BLES. *1998 Yearbook of Labor Statistics.* Bureau of Labor and Employment Statistics, Department of Labor and Employment, Manila, Philippines, 1998

DOLE-BLES. "The Labor Force Survey In Brief : January (1999-2000)." *LabStat,* Vol. 4 No. 6 March 2000

DOLE-Bureau of Labor Statistics. "Women in Employment: A Profile (1989-1999)," *LabStat,* Vol. 4 No. 4, February 2000

ECPAT. "Children Forced to Work," *ECPAT Bulletin,* Vol. 4/1, 1996-97

Flores-Oebanda, Ma. Cecilia, et al. *Child Domestic Workers: No Longer Out of Sight.* Visayan Forum Foundation: Manila, Philippines, 2000

Flores-Oebanda, Ma. Cecilia. "Child Domestic Workers in the Philippines," paper for the Girls' Invisible Labor Panel, presented in ILO conference 1998

Flores-Oebanda, Ma. Cecilia. "Conversations in Luneta Park," *Child Workers in Asia*. Vol 13. No. 1, pp. 22-23

Flores-Oebanda, Ma. Cecilia. "Girl Child in Invisible Labor: Child Domestic Workers in the Philippines," Visayan Forum Foundation: Manila, 1998

Flores-Oebanda, Ma. Cecilia. "Suffer the Silent Home Companions," presented in Geneva ILO Conference, June 1998

House Bill 8862, " 'Batas Kasambahay' or Magna Carta for Household Helpers." Republic of the Philippines House of Representatives: Quezon City, 7 December 1999

Ibarra, Teresita E. "Women Migrants, Focus on Domestic Helpers." *Philippine Sociological Review* No. 27, 1979, pp. 77-92

Illo, Jeanne Francis I., Ofreneo, Rosalinda Pineda, eds. *Carrying the Burden of the World: Women Reflecting on the Effects of the Crisis on Women and Girls*. UP Center for Integrative and Development Studies: Quezon City, Philippines, 1999

ILO/Department of Labor and Employment. *Child Labor: Let Us Work Against It*, 1996

ILO-IPEC. *Children in Hazardous Work in the Philippines*, 1999

ILO-IPEC. *IPEC Action Against Child Labor: Achievements, Lessons Learned and Indications for the Future (1998-1999)*. International Programme on the Elimination of Child Labour, International Labour Organization: Geneva, October 1999

Institute of Labor Studies. *Bata Man*. Vol. 2 No. 1, ILS: Manila, February 2000

Institute of Labor Studies. *Bata Man*. Vol. 2 No. 2, ILS: Manila, February 2000

International Labour Organization. *Attacking Child Labour in the Philippines: An Indicative Framework for Philippine-ILO Action*. ILO: Geneva, Switzerland, 1997

International Programme on the Elimination of Child Labour. "Highlights of the National Survey of Working Children - Philippines." 5 July 1997

Jimenez-David, Rina. "Magna Carta for househelp," *Philippine Daily Inquirer* 30 September 1999, p. 9

Jurado and Castro, 1978, cited by Romulo A. Virola in "Measuring the Contribution of the Informal Sector in the Philippines," *NSCB Technical Paper on the Informal Sector* No. 2001-003. NSCB: March 2001

Khan, Azizur Rahman. *Employment in a Globalizing and Liberalizing World.* International Labour Organization South-East Asia and the Pacific Multidisciplinary Advisory Team (SEAPAT): Manila, Philippines, 1997

Labor Code of the Philippines

Learnet Consulting, Inc. "The National Program Against Child Labor 2000-2004." 1 December 2000

Maggie Black and Jonathan Blagbrough of Anti-Slavery International. "First Things First." *innocenti digest 5.* UNICEF, 1999

Mante, James S. and Loree Cruz-Mante. *"Redefining the Strategic Directions and Thrusts of the National Program Against Child Labor 2000-2004,"* May 2001

National Statistical Coordination Board, 1992

National Statistics Office, Census 2000 Preliminary Results

National Statistics Office, Labor Force Survey, April 1995 cited by Ma. Alcestis A. Mangahas, *National NGO Consultation on CDWs in the Philippines,* 1996

National Statistics Office, Population Projections for 2001, Low Assumption

National Statistics Office, Labor Force Survey, April 1995

National Statistics Office, National Survey on Working Children, July 1995, Partial and Preliminary Results

Oledan, Radzini. "Magna Carta for house helpers garners support from NGOs," *The Philippine Post.* 11 April 2000, section A p. 5

Pacis, Roland. "Frequently Asked Questions on Child Domestic Workers in the Philippines," Visayan Forum Foundation: Manila, 1998

Pacis, Roland. "Just the maid," *Child Workers in Asia,* Vol 12, No. 3, CWA: 1997

Pacis, Roland. "Young Filipino househelpers plant the seeds of their freedom," *Child Workers in Asia.* Vol 16, No. 2, May-August 2000, pp. 3-5

Palanca, Clinton. "The Debate on Domestics." *Manila Times,* Nov. 21, 1995

Philippine Daily Inquirer, 1998

Rivera, Blanche S. "'*Kasambahay,*' not '*katulong*'," *Philippine Daily Inquirer* 27 April 2000, pp. 1 and 6

Salter, William D. *Children in Domestic Service: Preliminary Working Draft.* International Labour Organization, 1997

UNICEF. *innocenti digest* No. 5, 1999

Visayan Forum Foundation and Anti-Slavery International. Transcript of videotape: "Out of sight, out of mind," 1999

Visayan Forum Foundation. "Final Report of the Proceedings of the National NGO Consultation on Child Domestic Workers in the Philippines." Diliman, Quezon City, August 2-4, 1996

Visayan Forum Foundation. "Proceedings of the Regional Consultation on Child Domestic Workers in Asia." Diliman, Quezon City, November 19-24, 1997

Visayan Forum Foundation. "Women, Children and Internal Trafficking for Labor: A Situational Analysis at the Manila Port," April 2001

Visayan Forum Foundation. *Primer on Child Domestic Workers in the Philippines.* Manila, Philippines, 1999

Visayan Forum Foundation. *The Phenomenon of Child Domestic Work in Asia: Issues, Responses, and Research Findings.* (Background paper for the regional consultation in child domestic workers in Asia, 19-23 November 1997). Manila, Philippines, 1997

about the authors

Ma. Cecilia Flores-Oebanda

Cecil is the President of the Visayan Forum Foundation, Inc. She is also the current Chairperson of the Executive Board of Child Workers in Asia, as well as the Philippine and Southeast Asian Coordinator of the Global March Against Child Labor. One of the founding members of VF, she was instrumental in bringing VF into the forefront of the child labor movement in the Philippines. For the past 20 years, Cecil has been intensively involved with organizing, advocacy and campaigns with the urban poor, peasants, sugar plantation workers, youth and children. She was a political prisoner for 4 years under the Marcos dictatorship. She has four children: Eric, Kip, Malaya and Ani.

Roland Romeo R. Pacis

Roland is currently the Projects and Operations Manager of the Visayan Forum Foundation, Inc. He worked with VF since its establishment in the early 1990s, first as a student volunteer and later as full-time staff. Roland was also the Media Relations Officer of the Global March Against Child Labor's Philippine Secretariat, as well as a part of the Research, Documentation and Information-Dissemination Committee of Child Workers in Asia. Roland is a licensed Civil Engineer who graduated from the University of the Philippines-Diliman. He is currently taking up his Masters in Economics at the Asian Social Institute in Manila.

Virgilio P. Montaño

Vio is currently the Training Officer of the *Kasambahay* Program. He worked with the program since its inception in 1995. Vio is a member of the National Training Resource Pool for Child Labor that gives training on the design, management and evaluation of action programs on child labor. Like Roland, he was also a student volunteer during his college days. A Behavioral Science graduate of the University of the Philippines-Manila, Vio is married to Analyn Alvarez with whom he has a daughter, Avi.

about the VF staff

These are some of the people behind the Visayan Forum: its staff and volunteers who live for and with child domestic workers, their families and their communities. They are mainly based in Manila but more and more of them are in the regions. Individuals coming from different fields and backgrounds, they are bound together by a common calling, a mission. Co-pilgrims in this journey, in a shared dream: that working children shall fully enjoy their childhood; that everyone shall work for the benefit of all humanity. Working with dedication, hand-in-hand with partners, in this movement, in realizing this dream, in this generation.

seated: the authors (from left): Vio, Cecil, Roland; kneeling: Ben, Roger; standing: Edith, Jenefer, Mila, Marina, Gigi, Nene, Dhang, Jane, Ayen, Lillian & Jackie. Not in photo: Manila: Bea, Jerome, Angie, Lina, Tesing, Ester, May, Mila, Maribel; Batangas: Lolit, Marcia, Charo; Bacolod: Dane, Marlinee, Juliet, Araceli; Davao: Noreen, PJ, Dayana; CLASP: Kip, Vincent)